TRUMPET

TRUMPET

A N·o·v·e·l

TIM McLAURIN

W. W. NORTON & COMPANY New York London

The text of this book is composed in Bembo. Composition and
manufacturing by The Haddon Craftsmen, Inc.
Book design by Guenet Abraham.

Library of Congress Cataloging-in-Publication Data

McLaurin, Tim.
Woodrow's trumpet: a novel / by Tim McLaurin.—1st ed.
p. cm.
I. Title.
PS3563.C3843W66   1989
813'.54—dc19

ISBN 0-393-02701-5

W. W. Norton & Company, Inc.
500 Fifth Avenue, New York, N.Y. 10110

W. W. Norton & Company Ltd.
37 Great Russell Street, London WC1B 3NU

2 3 4 5 6 7 8 9 0

This book is dedicated with love and admiration to
Katie Early McLaurin
my wife and friend

TRUMPET

1

 chilly spring rain had been falling for two days when the clouds finally broke in the west. The fat lady slowly waddled from her purple and orange striped tent, detouring deep puddles, on her way to the hot dog stand where Ellis worked. Ellis spied the huge lady in her tent-like dress, and automatically took a couple of foot-long wiener buns from the steamer and began lathering them with chili. He was adding the onions when she sat down heavily on one of the stools, breathing as powerfully as if she had run a mile.

"Damn, Connie," Ellis said, squinting one eye and smiling.

"Baby doll, you know I would have brought you your supper in another thirty minutes. Get your feet wet?"

"No," Connie said between breaths. "I need the exercise anyhow." Her great bosom rose and fell.

The carnival was slow for opening night. Hard rain had kept the crowd away, and the only amusements going were the ones under shelter. Ellis watched a sliver of moon lick through the clouds. "Reckon things will pick up tomorrow?" he asked.

"Should, if the weather clears." Connie shredded a paper towel into a pile. She watched Ellis dice a bell pepper with the end of his spatula, the bits of vegetable popping on the hot, oiled grill. She liked the lanky boy with his quick smile and intense blue eyes. Sometimes he lingered at her tent after bringing supper, making small talk as if he shared her loneliness.

Connie sighed. "He knows, Ellis," she said quietly. "Frankie knows everything. They got into another fight and Joanie spilled her gut."

Ellis stiffened. He stirred the bits of bell pepper before shoveling them down the side of the bun. "Yeah? Knows what, Connie?"

"Don't play dumb with me, honey. I ain't blind."

"When did she tell him?"

"Only about thirty minutes ago. I heard them shouting inside their trailer."

Connie smiled sadly. She laid two dollars on the counter, took the wieners wrapped in white paper in one hand, pinched Ellis's cheek with the other, then turned and waddled away.

Ellis lay two more foot-longs on the grill. "Hey, Harry," he shouted to a man with tattoos and gray whiskers manning the other side of the tent. "I'm going to take a leak."

Ellis walked a quick, straight path through the midway to the small camper trailer he shared with Harry. Once inside, he locked the door, then began stuffing clothes into a battered canvas pack. Into his breast pocket, he slipped a plastic sack containing a few tablespoons of dirt. He gave the tiny room a once-over, then stooped through the door, checked left and right, and faded into the darkness beyond the circle of the midway. He considered slipping by to say so long to Connie, but decided the detour wasn't worth the possibility of getting caught.

Ellis had been with the carnival for six months, half of that time rotating as one of Joanie's lovers. Her husband owned the carnival, and Ellis knew if he stayed, he would certainly be out of a job, and more than likely, a couple pints of blood. In the feeble light from a camper window, Ellis counted his money. He swore at the thin stack of bills—a five, several ones—remembering tomorrow would have been payday. "Bitch wasn't even pretty," he mumbled.

The late May Tennessee night wasn't cold, just damp and chilly, the kind of weather that lay like cold sweat on his skin. Ellis zipped his denim jacket. He walked across a muddy field toward the bright glow of an overpass on nearby Interstate 40. The clay stuck to the tread of his tennis shoes, weighing his feet like bricks.

"Son of a bitch," Ellis mumbled. "Should have had better sense." He remembered at the end of the week the carnival would turn north for the summer tour of the New England states—a region he had yet to see.

Ellis reached a service road running parallel to the interstate. He scraped his soles on the edge of the asphalt, and looked back at the carnival glowing egg-shaped through the light mist.

Asshole probably stomping around after me right now, Ellis thought. He smiled. Several times he had seen Frankie consumed by jealous rage, stumbling the midway drunk and weeping, a razor weighing his pocket. Finally, Joanie would beg him home, the trailer would rock half the night, and the cycle would resume the next morning.

Ellis shouldered his pack and walked to the cloverleaf intersection. From the bridge, he first looked westward, then at the ribbon of concrete heading east. Few headlights traveled in either direction. The sign for a Holiday Inn shone a couple hundred yards away, but Ellis knew the night clerk would laugh at his nine dollars. He was contemplating a cold night huddled under the I-beams, when suddenly bright lights loomed, a semi braking for the eastbound entrance ramp. Ellis blinked as the beams crossed him, then heard the hiss of air brakes.

"Hey buddy," a man called from his high window. "You need a ride?"

Ellis searched the highway again, but saw no westbound traffic. "Where you heading?" he shouted.

"Carolina."

Ellis lifted his eyebrows. "As in North Carolina?"

"Square in the middle. University of North Carolina to be exact. I'm hauling desks."

Ellis felt his breath catch in his throat. He had to force his lungs to exhale. Heading home, he thought. I ain't wanting to go back there right now. But the rain is picking up and I'm tired and what the hell. It would hurt nothing to swing by the home place for a couple of hours, then head on for distant states—Oak Hills—that quiet, green community of his childhood, a place filled with memories so powerful they continued to haunt his dreams.

A thin red crack of dawn rolled back the dark sky in the east while Venus shimmered cold and blue above the treeline. Ellis stared at the morning through slitted eyelids as he rested against the seat, his mind whirling as he tried to remember where he was, whose truck he rode in. He turned his head slowly and stared at the driver as his recall of the night flooded back.

"Damn, man," Ellis apologized and sat up. "I didn't mean to conk out on you. Where we at?"

"About halfway between Burlington and Chapel Hill. Only a few more miles."

Ellis whistled. He rubbed his face. The air smelled of marijuana. "Reckon I wasn't much company. That last joint kicked my butt."

"Don't sweat it," the driver said, his eyes shiny from exhaustion and drugs. "I've done this run so many times, I can drive it asleep."

Ellis asked to be let out just outside Chapel Hill near the intersection that led to Oak Hills. The early dawn was cool and damp with fog. Ellis lit his last cigarette, trying to lift the dregs of sleep. He rode to Oak Hills with a potato chip delivery man.

The small township of Oak Hills was still quiet, the streets deserted of cars, when Ellis stepped from the truck. He turned in a slow circle, some of the shops familiar, some altered or replaced by new buildings. He spied the neon glow of a 7-Eleven that hadn't been there two years ago, and headed for it. The man behind the counter was yawning as Ellis pushed open the door. Ellis didn't know him. He bought a pack of Marlboros and a Pepsi and watched the storekeeper stifle another yawn while ringing up the sale.

"Hey, you didn't happen to know Woodrow, did you?" Ellis asked.

The man rubbed one eye. "Woodrow? He a psych major?"

Ellis chuckled, shaking his head. Woodrow would have liked that. "Naw. Not even close."

Ellis left the bright store, paused at the corner, then turned toward his old home. As he walked, he saw that Oak Hills had changed even more than he'd first realized, and though he had expected it, he was saddened. The old brick pharmacy was gone, the flower shop boarded up. Three old, wooden houses that had stood side by side had been leveled to make way for the foundation of a huge store. The old parallel parking spaces on each side of Main Street had been covered with new asphalt to widen the road. Ellis tossed the butt of his cigarette, then breathed deeply, but smelled new tar overpowering the good odor leaking from

Miss Penny's Bisquit Bar. He did hear the distant, lonely cry of a mourning dove.

At least it ain't all changed, he thought.

Ellis lengthened his gait, seeing that Venus was fading quickly against the dawn. He recalled how only a few years ago, he would already be walking beyond the town's boundary into farming land. The soil now nurtured clipped hedges that fronted new homes. Ellis paused before a large wooden sign that proclaimed,

WELCOME TO WHISPERING PINES

A COMMUNITY TO GROW WITH

Ellis studied the chiseled letters. The sign was gray and weathered as if it had stood for decades instead of probably a few months. He walked past the sign down a road he remembered being unpaved.

The morning turned. Venus was swallowed. As Ellis walked he listened to a growing chorus of birds, the chattering of two red squirrels as they raced down a tree trunk. He stopped, tilted his head, and listened. For a moment, from the ridge above town, he could swear he heard the strains of Woodrow's trumpet.

2

Eight-year-old Ellis frantically tugged at the knot joining the laces of his battered tennis shoes. Larry, two years older and the bully of dorm number two at Woodhaven Boys' Home, watched with a mean grin.

"Better hurry, pygmy," he said. "Gonna get left behind."

The front door opened and Wayne Enzor, a balding fifty-year-old man with pink, meaty cheeks, thrust his head and shoulders inside. "Ellis," he shouted. "Larry. Last call. I'm leaving in thirty seconds on the button and you two will be restricted for the day. Hear me?"

Larry smirked, then hurried past Enzor out the door. Ellis worked one loop of the knot free, unraveled the laces, and jammed his sneakers on. He raced outside, his face down and laces flapping, just as Enzor was starting the long, white van. Ellis squeezed onto the middle seat, the vehicle settling a little lower under the weight of fifteen squirming, shouting boys.

Saturday afternoon was a coveted time to the boys of the Home, for this was the day they went into the small town of Oak Hills for a couple of hours. Each of the fifty-odd boys in the Home performed chores to earn a weekly salary that ranged from a couple of quarters to several dollars. A dollar in the pocket of an eight-year-old was a fiery object, best cooled by an ice cream cone, soda pop, or the twilight of a matinee western.

Enzor walked around the van to close the sliding door, fussing under his breath while looking at his watch. He was on his third vanload of yelling kids.

"Quiet down," he shouted, sliding back under the driver's wheel, "else I ain't driving one foot."

Deathly silence for a quarter of a mile.

"Get off my hand."

"I ain't on your hand. Quit kicking my foot."

"I ain't kicking it."

"You're a liar."

"SHUT UP back there! I'll turn around this instant."

Deathly silence for a half mile.

"Where's my dollar? I've dropped my dollar." Low, mournful crying.

"Oh shut up, crybaby. Here's your old dollar."

"Quit elbowing me."

Hissing. "Then get off of my foot."

"I'll get you soon as we get out."

"I MEAN IT, BOYS. I'll turn around this instant and let every one of you spend the afternoon picking up trash."

The grind of down-shifted gears, squeal of brakes, a final shout from the boys as they greeted town.

Ellis and Teddy Baylor marched out the front door of Oak Hills Soda Shop, proudly holding aloft huge cones of chocolate ice cream. They studied the two blocks of shops and stores that constituted downtown Oak Hills: a theater, laundry, florist, two dry goods stores, pharmacy, Miss Penny's Bisquit Bar. Tall oaks and sweet gums shaded the cracked sidewalk.

"Look!" Ellis said, lifting one hand. At the end of the business district where green front lawns began, a crowd was gathered.

"Dogfight!" Teddy shouted. He raced down the street. Ellis followed, holding his cone aloft like a blazing torch, weaving between curious people walking toward the commotion.

Ellis ran into a wall of legs. He was small, a good three inches shorter than the other boys his age, but with deft maneuvering, he crawled, slipped, and squeezed his way to the front.

Not a dogfight in sight. Not even two dogs in love. Ellis looked from side to side in bewilderment, before noticing everyone was looking above their heads. Ellis followed their gaze.

A man sat ten feet above the ground in the fork of a chinaberry tree. His face was pressed against the bark, thick muscular arms wrapped nearly around the forked trunk. The big man's body shook with sobs. He was buck naked. Ellis dropped his ice cream cone.

"It's a shame, ain't it?" Ellis heard an adult say. "War do that to a grown man."

"Naw. Vietnam didn't do it," another adult argued. "He wasn't over there two months. Woodrow's been queer his whole life."

Ellis mourned his ice cream melting into the grass, then stared back at the man huddled in the tree. He knew of Woodrow. The Bunce family were big farmers and the wealthiest people in Oak Hills. Gossip was a favorite pastime in the community, especially concerning the Bunces. Ellis had heard the story of Woodrow's birth time and again from a black midwife who doubled as a laundress at the Home.

"Lord, Lord," the midwife always told it, "dat child come into the world right queer from the start. Twelve years after his second brother, when his mother thought she was done with birthin'. Big pumpkin head like you never see on a baby. Liked to split his mama open. And dem shoulders, wide as a two-year-old. I had to take a razor to poor Mrs. Bunce, and den he come shooting out and was smiling. Believe me, 'cause the Lord knows I ain't lying. Covered with his mama's blood with that same ole moon-faced smile he tote the rest of his life. Weren't no more concerned than if he was on a hayride. Weren't even crying, not one sound, so I pick him up by his feet and smacked his hinny and his ole chest rise up, but still no sound. I've birthed hogs to humans and ain't seen the beat since."

At birth, Woodrow weighed fourteen pounds two ounces, the largest child ever born in the county, and by age sixteen stood at six foot four with arms as thick as most people's legs.

Ellis saw the big man turn his head slightly to look at the mob, then shut his eyes tight. He felt strangely sad and ashamed for Woodrow. He remembered seeing him at church and around town, either alone or with one of his older brothers, never speaking and looking like a kicked dog.

"Benson's gonna have to cart him off for good this time," Ellis heard another adult say. "Must be a heartache for them."

"Shit," someone else said in a lower voice. "The only thing that would give a Bunce a heartache is if the banks were to fail."

Ellis heard a murmur at the rear of the crowd. The chatter ceased as two men around forty pushed their way to the front. The first was Benson Bunce, the short and stocky oldest brother, followed by Porter, a taller, stoop-shouldered man wearing spectacles. Both had been the first sons of Oak Hills to attend college and had earned medals in Korea.

"Yeah, it's Woodrow, all right," Benson hissed over his shoulder to Porter. He spread his legs and clasped his hands over his hips. "Damn it all, Woodrow. God damn it."

SUMMER 1979

Frogs chirped in full chorus from the mossy shore of the irrigation pond. Two crows fussed from the top of a pine tree. The air was hot and thick, low thunder threatening from dark clouds on the western horizon.

Slap, slap, slap, three heavy-bosomed black women grabbed handfuls of tobacco leaves held by youngsters and looped the leaves by their stems to pine sticks supported upon a frame.

"Stick!" one looper shouted, her nimble fingers knotting the twine, then snapping it. A small boy struggled to lift the forty-pound bundle. The looper stood impatiently holding an empty stick to be placed on the frame.

"Stick!" another looper shouted. The boy was slow. "Move that stick, youngun," she scolded, "and get it in the barn. Can't you hear that thundercloud rolling up?"

Thirteen-year-old Ellis lounged against the tire of a John Deere tractor. His flannel shirt was dark with sweat, and black tobacco gum coated his hands and forearms where his sleeves were rolled up. "Tote that stick, boy," he shouted. The stick toter turned and stuck out his tongue. Ellis grinned. With one fist he rubbed the soreness in his lower back.

Ellis was working his first summer as a cropper, nearly a man, none of that baby stuff working at the barn with the women and children. He flaunted his exhaustion like a medal. Early that morning, the sun only a half globe against the treeline, he had felt dread standing at the head of a quarter-mile row of wet stalks. But the tractor cranked, he had sucked in his breath, bent low, and waded in, gasping at the cold, July dew, snapping the three or four yellowing leaves from the bottom of each stalk, tucking them under his armpit till he had a load to place in the trailer, stems out, then bending again, his muscles slowly warming and stretching, working hard to keep his row even with the tractor. Cropping was a man's job, and it was now his privilege to lounge against the tractor while waiting for an empty trailer.

"Get the lead out of your britches," Ellis shouted again at the young stick toter. The boy was from the Home, a resident of dorm two. He mouthed an obscenity at Ellis.

" 'Bout time Woodrow gets back," Ellis said to James, a black cropper his own age.

James was rubbing dirt on the gum covering his hands. "Yeah, 'bout time old pie face gets on back," he answered.

One of Woodrow's chores was bringing cold sodas and packs of cheese nabs to the workers at mid-afternoon. The caffeine and sugar pumped you up after long hours laboring under a hot sun.

An old woman handing tobacco leaves to the looper suddenly broke into the first verse of "Shall We Gather at the River." Two other women joined in, but the song died after the first stanza. The youngsters didn't know the words. They enjoyed the music on the radio now, not the old hymns from church. The old woman hummed the second verse alone.

Ellis heard the growl of a motor gearing down and turned, expecting to see Woodrow and Benson Bunce returning to the barn. Instead, a long, low white car swung into the dusty drive.

The late-model Lincoln crept forward over the roots and ruts. Ellis stared at paint waxed to the luster of a pearl, twin chromed exhaust pipes, tinted windshield glass. The car stopped twenty yards from the barn in the shade of an oak.

Soon, the passenger door swung open, and two long, coffee-colored legs appeared, a bright, red skirt riding high on her

thighs, exposing a glimpse of white panties. Ellis felt a flutter low
in his bowels. James climbed on the rim of the tractor tire to get a
better look.

The young black woman was tall and slender, only a few
pounds shy of skinny, but with proud breasts that rode high and
pointy and buttocks that stretched the fabric of her skirt. Her lips
were painted red, her hair ironed straight and slicked until it
shone blue-black under the sun.

"Who the fuck is that?" Ellis whispered.

James's brow was furrowed, his ears pulled forward. His
Adam's apple bobbed. "Nadean," he replied. "Nadean Tucker."

Ellis had heard of Nadean from Miss Essie, her mother, who
had cooked at the Home for fifteen years. Ellis recalled her many
sermons on the daughter she had lost to the sin and vice of
Washington, D.C., after she ran off from home at sixteen.

Ellis studied the woman. She was what local whites called a
"high yeller," her skin the shade of a paper grocery sack. She
lifted her chin, narrowing one eye at the staring, dusty tobacco
laborers.

Except for a grumble of far-off thunder, silence reigned. Finally Mattie Turner said, "Nadean, gal, you better come on over
here."

She came strutting, a smile parting her lips to show even, white
teeth. Her tall heels sank in the sand, so Nadean flipped them off
and continued barefoot, wiggling like a black snake.

James talked low in his throat. "Uh-huh. What I wouldn't do
for a mess of that."

Ellis felt himself blush. Here he was staring at a black woman.
He turned his eyes, but only for a moment.

A murmur passed through the crowd. A teenaged black girl
dropped her handful of leaves and ran to meet Nadean. They
hugged, a farm laborer in her stained, loose cotton frock, holding
to a creature as brightly colored and fragile as a bird.

"Cousin Nadean," the girl shouted. "What you doing back home?" Suddenly, aware of her sap-coated hands, the girl backed away and dropped her head. Nadean reached down and tousled the girl's hair.

"Hey there, honey. Now ain't you growing into a pretty thing."

Nadean looked up at the crowd staring at her. "Well, can't no more of you niggers say hello to a home girl?" Nadean cocked one hand on her hip. A gold-capped tooth glittered between her lips. "Ya'll think I ain't never worked in tobacco?"

As Nadean posed, her feet wide, a bottom button on her skirt popped open. James choked. Ellis's eyes moved up and down the woman's legs. Suddenly, several more young women broke from the crowd and rushed to meet Nadean.

"How it be in D.C.?"

"Girl, what you doing in that big, fine car?"

"Lord, I couldn't imagine who in the world was driving up."

Nadean leaned to kiss several of the women, but none would hug her. They hid their hands, while staring at Nadean's long, red nails, the sparkling rings on three of her fingers.

The driver's door of the car opened; a tall black man rose and peered over the roof. He wore a white suit with a broad-brimmed, white leather hat.

Big-shot jig, Ellis thought.

The man stared over the top of his shades for several seconds, then, as if disgusted by what he saw, pushed up his shades and slipped back into the car. After several seconds, he tooted the horn.

Nadean moved through the crowd, stopping to hug someone, slap another on the back. The young croppers inched forward. The men hanging tobacco inside the barn came outside. Once when Nadean bent to hug a small girl, the edge of her panties showed, prompting a round of whistles and coughing.

Woodrow and Benson returned with the sodas. Benson drove

slowly past the long car. The man tooted his horn again. Nadean lifted one hand and nodded.

Benson took his time getting from the cab of the truck, studying Nadean, then the big car. Work had ceased since Nadean's arrival, and the older women motioned for people to get back to work. The trailor should have already been emptied and the croppers on their way back to the field. "Stick," one of the loopers shouted. She jerked at a young boy's arm and motioned him to get going.

Benson set the case of sodas on a stump. He cut his eyes at Nadean. "Let's get going now," he shouted toward the workers. "Damn baccor is burning up in the field."

Nadean took several steps closer to where Woodrow and Benson stood. "How you doing, Mr. Bunce?" she asked. "You remember when I used to work for you?"

Benson nodded briskly, then busied himself popping the caps on the bottles.

Nadean turned to Woodrow. "How you doing, Mr. Woodrow?"

Woodrow smiled, blushed, and stared at the dirt.

"Well, I reckon I better be going and let ya'll get on back to work," Nadean said loudly. "Wouldn't want Mr. Bunce's tobacco to burn up in the field. Hell, no."

Walking to the car, Nadean seemed intent on getting maximum movement from her backside. Benson watched from the corner of his eye. Woodrow pretended to study the ground.

"Bye, ya'll," Nadean shouted, then slid behind the tinted glass.

The gossip that continued that afternoon was hotter than the summer sun.

Older women:

"She's a shame and heartache to her mama. Nearly killed Essie, it did."

"Girl raised in the church and dress now like she right fresh off the street corner."

"You expect anything different? She dat way, what I hear, when she was little. See the way she was looking at dem young boys?"

Young women in whispers:

"Lord Jesus, if there be a heaven it got to be in D.C."

"I bet she in the movies. Rae said she heard she's working in the movies with Billy Dee."

"You see that car? Could'a put our whole house in there and have room left over."

"Granny say she's a sinner. Lord, let me live long enough to sin."

Men in the field:

"I'd hang something in her so fast, she think she been hit by lightning."

"Shit, gal fine as her not let a poor-ass fool like you close enough to smell it."

"Shit you talk."

"Hey, Ellis. You still got a hard-on? You ain't got to be 'shamed of it 'cause you white."

Ellis under his breath: "Damn black whore."

"Ya'll see that old big-headed Woodrow? I thought his tongue was gonna fall out of his mouth."

Slap went the rhythm of the leaves. The workers hurried to fill the barn while the lingering thundercloud grumbled a warning.

3

llis's eyes opened to frost flowers decorating the windowpane beside his bed. He lay still, wondering what had awakened him—maybe a burglar with a knife, maybe just one of the other fellows coughing. He peeped over the edge of the covers and searched the dim light inside the dorm. Then, from far into the fields and woods, he heard the long, low blast of a horn.

Woodrow, Ellis thought. Crazy fucker is hunting again.

The cry of the horn lasted for more than five seconds, seemed to roll down from the hilly country north of town, building in volume like a landslide. Woodrow's four bluetick hounds bayed deep-throated back at the horn.

Must be freezing out there, Ellis thought, pulling his blanket to just below his eyes. That Woodrow is one weird bird.

Often on winter nights when most people in Oak Hills were sleeping, Woodrow ran his hounds through fields and along the ridges outside of town. He had raised the pups on a baby bottle after the bitch was killed by a car and had trained them to obey both his voice and blasts from his hollow hunting horn. When Woodrow first began hunting not long after his release from the mental hospital, there was lots of speculation by townspeople as to what prompted him to run behind four hounds until the early morning hours. For a man who had lived his entire life following the orders of others, the hunts were strangely out of character. But as time passed, the hunts became just another facet of a man no one really understood, another side of his craziness. Woodrow was harmless. Let him hunt. The duet between his horn and hounds was heard only by the sleepless—a man getting up to empty his bladder, a mother sitting in watch over a fevered child, Ellis staring at frost flowers.

The hounds turned their path, their baying slowly becoming louder. Again the horn sounded, beginning flat but rising in pitch, lifted at the end and cut cleanly as if split with a knife. The hounds raged in reply, the sound dreamlike and haunting.

Ellis took his eyes from the dark window and pulled the covers higher where he could only see from one eye. "Buddy," he said to the boy sleeping on the rack above him. His voice was muffled by the covers. Ellis lifted his foot and kicked the bottom of the mattress. "Buddy," he hissed. "You asleep?"

Buddy mumbled, then rolled to his side. Silence. Ellis coughed to hear noise. He listened to the collection of snores and sighs coming from various beds in the long room. The hunt frightened him. The sound was so lonely, as lonely as the hoot of an owl, a whippoorwill—even lonelier than that—like trying to imagine eternal life, a clock ticking in a silent room, the sound of his pulse in his ear late at night. Ellis pictured in his mind bare winter branches, old houses void of furniture, cracked, thrown-away shoes.

Once when the hounds had swung especially close to the Home. Ellis had spied Woodrow's electric lantern shining across a far pasture, swinging from side to side like a beacon. For a moment he wondered if Woodrow was trying to signal him and tell him something that was important to know—something other people in Oak Hills had never known or had long forgotten.

Naw, Woodrow doesn't know nothing other people don't know, Ellis reasoned. Probably not as much, simpleminded as he is.

The hunt was reaching a climax. Whatever the hounds were chasing, they were gaining on it. Their baying was frantic, Woodrow's horn splitting the frigid air every fifteen seconds. Ellis turned on his side and hiked the covers completely over his head, leaving only an air hole to breathe through.

Let's see, got a literature test tomorrow, he thought, trying to ignore the thump of his heart. Who wrote *One Flew Over the Cuckoo's Nest*?

The hounds screamed as a long blast from Woodrow's horn turned the hunt up a hill and over a ridge. A curtain of earth absorbed their baying. Ellis heard one last thin trumpet blast before dropping under a blanket of sleep.

SUMMER 1982

Miss Essie said the unusually heavy growth of sweet-gum seed burrs was an omen. The spiny, green balls grew in such abundance that large branches would snap and crash to the ground in still weather. Cars lost windshields, and a cow died

when her back was broken. Several farmers lost their tobacco
crop when heavy hail fell from an unusual thunderstorm that
rolled in from the east. "Bad omens," said Miss Essie.

The failed tobacco crop prompted Benson Bunce and a couple
other farmers to yield to a persistent realty company and sell land
to be developed into a subdivision on the outskirts of Oak Hills.
The growth of the university, the completion of a nearby research park, and the mild, North Carolina climate had combined
to draw new homeseekers from all over the country. Benson sold
seventy-five acres, land that his great-grandfather had bought and
planted.

Then Amma Bunce died from a stroke in August after chasing
chickens out of her flower bed, the last founding member of the
township to pass on.

Mournful organ music poured from the open front door of the
Oak Hills Baptist Church. The congregation slowly filed in,
dressed in their best dark suits and dresses. The long, black hearse
gleamed under a high sun. Ellis shuffled his feet while standing in
line. His shoes were too tight and hurt his toes; sweat rolled in
slow trains down his face.

"I'm going to choke to death," Ellis whispered to the boy
standing in front of him. He pulled at the thin, brown tie knotted
around his neck.

"Old bitch would have to die in summer," the boy whispered.

Enzor noticed Ellis's fidgeting, walked over, and stared down
at him through narrowed eyes.

The boys of the Home occupied a special section of the pews,
strategically located in the center of the church under the severe
eyes of deacons and Sunday school teachers. They shuffled slowly
through the arched front door, onto the worn, red carpet, the first
boy in line, then each in turn, sighting the pastoral scene of Christ
with two lambs backdropping the pulpit, the sprays of bright

carnations and lilies set in a semicircle—then with horror—the gray-and-silver casket, the side of Mrs. Bunce's gray head, her face tilted toward the ceiling.

The first boy balked, causing a domino chain of collisions. Enzor cleared his throat and nudged the boy forward. The sight of the dead woman gave Ellis the sudden urge to spit, as if even the air filling the church were dead and stagnant. He moved on wooden legs to his place on the bench. He sat in the middle, five pews from the front, almost even with the side of her face.

She don't look dead, Ellis thought. That bothered him most of all. In his nightmares, dead people had looked ghoulish with green skin and fiery red eyes. The dead dogs and squirrels he had encountered had been dismembered and broken. Mrs. Bunce looked like she was only napping. Her white hair was combed, her cheeks powdered, her lips tinted pink. Could a person just slip from life into death that easily, he wondered? Could he just as easily one night stop breathing in his sleep?

The church was full. Even a few blacks who had worked for the Bunces were sitting in the back row. The organist played "Amazing Grace," "Shall We Gather at the River," and "Uncloudy Day"—one mournful song after another until everyone was seated. The minister stood towering over the casket behind the pulpit.

"Brothers and sisters," he began. "We have gathered here today to pay our last respects to a woman who is now with God."

Ellis heard a gasp, saw a woman sitting in the family pew cover her face with a handkerchief. The three Bunce brothers sat in the front row, Woodrow leaning forward with his head cradled in his hands.

"And one day we shall all have to stand before our maker," the preacher shouted. "Before God in all his glory. Will you be ready like Amma Bunce was ready?"

Ellis was hard pressed to feel remorse. As long as he could remember, Enzor had used Amma Bunce's name to inject humility into the boys living in the Home. "You should be more thankful for what you have, for the people who care about you," he liked to say. "If it wasn't for the money Mrs. Bunce gives to this home each year, we might have to close down." Every time he found a ball lying around or a cracked bat, he would start in again. "You boys don't appreciate anything. Here, the Bunces made it possible for us to build a ball field and buy new equipment, and you leave it lying around like it was garbage." I don't even like baseball, Ellis thought bitterly.

Ellis mouthed the words to another hymn, hung his head as the preacher prayed long and fervently, and hoped that a person had to be at least as old as Mrs. Bunce to slide so easily into death. "She was a woman loved by young and old," he heard the preacher say. Ellis recalled conversations he had overheard about how tightfisted the old woman was—how she used her money to control Oak Hills.

At the close of the prayer, the first rows of people began to file across the front of the church, passing before Mrs. Bunce. Ellis felt small knots grab in his stomach. Walk right beside her? Within touching distance? He wished Enzor wasn't such a hawk and he could slip to the opposite aisle and join the line of people exiting the church.

Ellis glanced ahead into her face for only a moment, then fixed his eyes on the belt loop of the person in front of him. From the corner of his eye, he saw adults reach and touch her folded hands. Ellis shuffled forward like a blind man.

Woodrow sobbed into his palms. Benson and Porter sat against the back of the bench as grim as marble statues, nodding at words of condolence.

Ellis was startled to see the big man crying. Except for the day in the tree, he had never seen Woodrow show more emotion than a thin smile. Today, his wide shoulders heaved, his hair was ruffled, and down his face coursed twin tracks of tears. A few people placed their hand on his shoulder, but most averted their eyes. As Ellis passed, he had a sudden urge to reach and touch Woodrow, comfort him in the way he might a whimpering puppy. There has to be pain with death, Ellis decided with relief. Someone has to hurt for you, to cry, even if he is a simpleton. Ellis recalled the times he had seen road killed animals, and always the mate dog or possum or racoon hovered nearby, sometimes even getting killed in attempts to retrieve the carcass. Hadn't he seen a mother squirrel once chattering and scolding as she tried to carry the cold body of her baby back up the tree to the nest. Hadn't he heard cows and hogs lowing and squealing when one of their herd was being prepared for slaughter. People now cried for Mrs. Bunce, a conniving woman silly enough to kill herself chasing chickens from a flower bed.

Ellis could not imagine anyone who would suffer over his own death. Certainly not Enzor. Not a single one of the fellows in the Home. His real mother wouldn't even know it if he died. Ellis decided that if he stayed out of the way of large trucks and shotguns, that if he didn't get silly over chasing chickens off a piece of ground, and if he didn't get close enough to someone for them to mourn his passing, he should be safe for quite a few years. Something as important as dying had to have some rules about it. A person couldn't just slip out of himself as he lay alone, staring at the ceiling some dark night.

Ellis shuffled down the aisle, closer and closer to the casket. As he was passing the body, he felt a magnetism flowing from her that made him turn his head and look. Yes, she was dead and far beyond sleep, the way her eyes had sunk back into the sockets, her lips thin and dried of blood, the skin covering her face already molding to the bones of her skull—all belied she was only resting. She was dead. The sobs guaranteed it. Ellis squinted his eyes until her powdered face was only a blur, then bent quickly and pressed his lips to her cold cheek. The boys behind him gasped and faltered in step. From the corner of his eye, Ellis saw Enzor's tight frown. He marched forward and focused his eyes on sunlight brighter than silver flooding the front door.

Amma Bunce's will was read one week after her burial. Six hundred and fifty acres of prime farmland and forest, machinery, tenant houses, and assets were divided equally between Benson and Porter.

Woodrow fared much poorer. His inheritance was a scant five hilltop acres and a modest four-room frame house. The property around had been sold off to developers. Woodrow also was granted for life a monthly thousand-dollar trust income to be administered by Porter.

Woodrow, in his usual manner, seemed not at all bothered by the inequality of his inheritance. He complained to no one, did not even speak of the will. Many of the citizens of Oak Hills wondered if he even cared about money and property any more than he seemed to care about sports or the events of the surrounding world.

The last load of cured tobacco was carried to market in Durham in late September. Without a word to anyone, Woodrow rose early two mornings later, gathered a few clothes, loaded his hounds in the bed of his pickup, and drove the couple of miles to his property. Woodrow Bunce had been reborn in the autumn of his thirty-fifth year.

FEBRUARY 1983

Emboldened by his new theory on the prerequisites for death, Ellis waded in and punched the next fellow who kidded him about his height.

The punch landed solid, a satisfying smack against Jamie Wade's belly. He bent double, gasped, cussed, then yelled at the top of his wind. The dorm attendant came running, then hauled Ellis before Enzor, who restricted him to the grounds for the next three weekends.

Ellis often wondered what unknown sin he had committed to be cursed to stand only five feet seven inches when most of the other fellows at age seventeen stood at least an inch taller. Daily he measured his height against the ruler tacked to the bathroom wall, but no change had occurred since the sixth grade. His chest and legs were as smooth as eggshells, his voice still the tenor of a child. Many of the girls at school were taller than he was.

Another distinction that separated Ellis from most other boys in the Home was the fact that he was a bastard and ward of the state. Ellis had no real idea where he came from, just a couple of splintered memories. Most of the other fellows had living parents or family who for varying reasons could not or would not keep them. Most had their full tuition, or a large part of it, paid for by their family, and most received letters, gifts on birthdays and Christmas, and an occasional visit.

But Ellis was well cared for. He could not remember once when a lost tooth did not return a quarter. He had presents to open on holidays, pats on the head from Enzor, and hugs from Miss Essie. The Home took care of his basic needs, even if he was cursed never to grow, and even if he could not remember once someone saying they loved him.

"I'll catch up with them cocksuckers," Ellis mumbled, lying on his rack with his face buried in a pillow. "Give them all hell, too." He mourned that he would miss the carnival next weekend. And the new Clint Eastwood movie would be long gone before he was allowed back in town.

The front door to the dorm swung open. "On line, fellows," Enzor shouted as he walked in. He stood ramrod straight, the result of twenty years' service in the army. His father and grandfather had served as director of the Home before him.

What the heck now, Ellis wondered as he swung off the rack and lined his toes with the red stripe that ran down each side of the dorm. Other boys grumbled as they hurried to take their place.

Woodrow followed Enzor through the door, a sight that started more grumbling between the boys. The visit of a Bunce, usually Benson, meant one thing—the need of farm labor at below minimum wages.

Enzor cleared his throat twice to quiet the dorm. His eyes were owlish as they swept the room. Woodrow towered behind him.

"Boys, I know any one of you would be glad to volunteer your help to Mr. Bunce. The pool built last year was the direct result of the Bunce family's generosity. Unfortunately, he only needs one worker."

Woodrow took a half step to Enzor's side where Ellis could see him better. He was dressed in his usual overalls and heavy brogans, but something about him today was different. Ellis cocked his head, wondering, then realized that Woodrow wasn't looking at the ground. His face was lifted, and he was staring up and down the row of boys.

"Boys, Mr. Bunce is getting ready to plant spring crops and needs some dependable labor to help some afternoons after school and on weekends. This will be an excellent opportunity for one of you older boys to earn some money, while learning the value of good, hard work."

Ellis groaned. He still vividly remembered the low back pain he had suffered bent double cropping tobacco. Enzor and Woodrow began walking down the line. Occasionally Enzor pointed at one of the boys while whispering to Woodrow.

As the two men approached, Ellis tucked in his chin and tried to appear as short as possible. He stared at the floor. Woodrow passed him, then suddenly stopped and took a step backwards.

"What's your name, son?" Woodrow asked.

Ellis kept his eyes to the floor, hoping that Woodrow was addressing another. After a moment of silence, followed by a harsh clearing of the throat by Enzor, Ellis peeked and found Woodrow's eyes meeting his own.

"Ellis," he croaked. "Ah, Ellis McDonald." He added a quick "sir" when Enzor cleared his throat again.

With words as slow as backwater Woodrow said, "You want to work with me?"

Ellis was surprised at Woodrow's voice. Rarely had he heard him speak, and then only a mumbled yes or no to orders from Benson, preferring to use only a nod of his head instead of talking. But today, he spoke strong and rich like the clanging of a large bell. Ellis understood now how the blast from Woodrow's hunting horn carried for miles.

Enzor put his hand on Woodrow's shoulder and led him to the middle of the dorm. He talked low, but vigorously. Ellis heard the word "troublemaker." Woodrow shook his head, then turned away. Enzor followed him, frowning. Ellis had to crane his head way back to look the big man in his face.

"I remember you from last summer," Woodrow said. "You work hard. Want a job?"

Ellis definitely didn't want a job, but after hearing Enzor's criticism, he thrust his chin forward and nodded. "Yeah. Yes, sir. I would like to work." He cut his eyes at Enzor.

Woodrow nodded. "Pick you up early Saturday." He turned and walked from the dorm without another word.

With the eastern sky only faintly pink, Ellis sat huddled on the front steps waiting for Woodrow. The late February morning was cold, his breath hanging before him in a white cloud. No birds called, no doves, the frogs and crickets and robins still a month away. Ellis hugged his knees and wished he was still in bed, and had never laid eyes on Woodrow Bunce.

Ellis thought again of the couple who had come the night before to see him. They looked at me like they were at the dog pound or something, he recalled. It's a wonder they didn't ask to see my shot chart. Years back, he had hoped one of the couples would take him home, had even cried after some left and never returned. Now, he just wanted to turn eighteen and be on his own.

"Fuck that bitch," Ellis mumbled, remembering how the woman had asked if he wanted to be her boy. "Ellis McDonald ain't nobody's boy." He had told her that, right to her pig face. "No. I want to stay right here."

Ellis took a cigarette from inside the lining of his coat and lit it. Getting caught smoking was a paddling, plus a month's grounding, but most of the older boys took the risk. He blew a stream of smoke toward the gathering dawn, then cupped the glowing ash between his palms. Wonder what in the world he's gonna have me doing? Way too early for tobacco.

The first glint of sunlight was visible through the tree branches when Ellis heard the down-shifting of gears, then saw Woodrow turning his Ford pickup into the driveway of the Home. Ellis stomped out his second cigarette and stood.

"Morning," Woodrow said, leaning to open the passenger door. Ellis returned the greeting while climbing onto the seat.

"You ate?" Woodrow asked.

"Naw. Ain't hungry," Ellis said.

Woodrow drove back onto the road and headed toward Oak Hills. He stopped in front of Miss Penny's place.

"Can't work hungry," Woodrow said. He went inside and returned in a few minutes with a paper sack containing ham bisquits and two cups of coffee. They ate in silence while Woodrow slowly drove the last half mile to his property.

Ellis was surprised at the appearance of Woodrow's home. During the years the house was rented out, the yard had grown over with scrub bushes, the walls had peeled until they were gray. Now, the jumble of weeds and bushes had been cleared, the dead grass burned off. Woodrow had painted the house bright yellow with white window trim.

Woodrow had been in the house for five months. His decision

to leave had caused a family stir. Benson had assumed that Wood-row would continue to live with him and his wife and kids in the big family house, handy to the many chores that go with running a farm. When Woodrow refused Benson's orders to return home, the two older brothers decided to wait him out, figuring he would tire of living alone after a couple of months. Certainly he would return to what senses he possessed in time for tobacco planting in May.

Ellis wondered why Woodrow had stopped here. The farm was still miles down the road. Maybe he forgot something? Woodrow stepped from the truck, then motioned for Ellis to come. Ellis followed his long strides around the side of his house to the backyard. Woodrow's hounds yelped at the sight of their master.

Ellis had often wondered about these night hunters. Their long bays from the ridgeline, heard in the quiet of midnight, were wolfish. Ellis expected to see rawboned animals with narrow, gleaming eyes. He found a speckled bitch standing against the wire wagging her tail, sleek and fat with happy brown eyes. The other hounds turned in circles, yelped, and flashed dog grins.

"They bite?" Ellis asked. Woodrow shook his head. Ellis rubbed the bitch through the wire. She licked his hand. Another hound walked over, wagging from the neck back, begging to be rubbed.

Woodrow dragged a garden hose to the pen, then filled a concrete trough with water. While Ellis rubbed the dogs, Wood-row gazed over the four-acre field behind his house. He started walking toward the center of the field, Ellis following. The field had not been plowed or mowed for years and was grown over with broom straw, scrubby pine saplings, and sassafras. Woodrow trampled a wide path in the brush; Ellis stumbled over the stalks and vines.

Woodrow stopped in the center of the field, then turned to scout the boundaries of his small domain. Ellis followed his gaze.

Ellis thought Woodrow's property to be much like an island. The land was on a hill, surrounded on three sides by the new subdivision. Most of the half-acre lots not already under construction were being marked off with stakes and string, or being cleared by chain saw and bulldozer. Ellis was surprised at the rapid growth of the subdivision. Five houses were already completed and lived in, another ten or so under way. The closest house was less than a hundred yards from Woodrow's. He recalled that the first lot had been sold almost a year ago.

"Lot of work to be done," Woodrow stated.

What work, Ellis wondered? He ain't planning on farming this scrap of land, is he?

"Yeah, lot of work." Woodrow kneeled and dug his fingers into the dirt. He scooped out a handful of soil, then pressed it into a cake. He held the soil to his nose, breathing in deeply the pungent smell. "Good dirt. Ain't been spoiled."

Ellis took the cake of earth when Woodrow passed it, sniffed as the big man had done, but did not understand. Dirt was dirt. Why does he want to grow tobacco in this little field, Ellis wondered? Time you get started down a row, it will be time to turn around.

Ellis watched Woodrow study various sections of the field, prod the earth with his foot, poke it, even touch a clod of soil to his tongue. He had never known a person to stare so intently, as if he were seeing something below the weeds that was invisible to others.

"Ain't you worried about trucking the tobacco so far to the barn?" Ellis ventured.

Slowly, Woodrow turned from his daydream. "What?"

"It's a good two miles to the nearest of your tobacco barns. You ain't worried about a lot of leaves blowing off the trailer?"

Woodrow shook his head. "No. I ain't growing tobacco no more."

"You ain't? Well, why you talking about clearing this field?"

"Gonna grow watermelons," Woodrow answered. "Big watermelons."

Ellis squinted one eye. He stared at the hole Woodrow had dug with his boot toe. "Watermelons?" No one in Oak Hills grew more than a few vines of watermelons in the corner of their garden. Why would anyone plant four acres, for God's sake? This sucker is crazy as people say.

Woodrow returned to his daydream. Ellis shook his head and chuckled. Four acres of watermelons. For some reason, the image made him happy.

or two weeks, Ellis helped Woodrow for a couple of hours after school, and all day Saturday, cutting the saplings with bush axes and piling them in the center of the field. In the beginning, Ellis struggled to handle the long ax, but by the end of the third day could nearly keep pace with Woodrow. Woodrow made no concession to Ellis's size, and Ellis worked hard to justify his confidence.

The field was set with fire on a windless afternoon in mid-March. Before lighting it, Woodrow spent an hour combing the field searching for rabbit nests. He found three and carefully scooped up the young in their beds of down, hiding them in the edge of the woods. Ellis was amazed to see the mother rabbits follow hopping at Woodrow's feet, no more afraid of him than if he were a cow or horse. The line of flames crept across the dry stubble, held in check by the wet burlap sacks Woodrow and Ellis had set at the edge of the field. The piles of saplings were dry, and burned fiercely, throwing twenty-foot flames into the sky. The smoke prompted several carloads of curious people to drive by, and Harold Culver, the captain of the volunteer fire department, stopped briefly to see that everything was under control. After the fires had died to beds of smoking, white ash, Woodrow and Ellis walked the border of the field, beating out any last fingers of flame.

"Fire will put potash back in the soil," Woodrow explained. Ellis nodded. That was usually the extent of conversation between the two, a few words, a nod. Ellis still thought Woodrow to be every bit as crazy as people said, but was beginning to like him. Ellis was especially pleased with his wages—three dollars and a half an hour, nearly double what he had been paid in the tobacco fields.

Ellis saved his money by hiding it in a sock that he stuffed in his underwear. As required by Enzor, he gave a tithe of ten percent to the church every Sunday, but he minimized the damage by lying about how much he was paid.

A few afternoons after they had burned off the field, Ellis reported to Woodrow and found a small Farmall tractor and disk parked at the edge of the field. By nightfall, Woodrow had taught him to plow a reasonably straight furrow. Next day, they began cultivating the ground, Ellis driving the tractor while Woodrow plodded behind, breaking up large clots with a hoe. The field was plowed, limed, then plowed and hoed again until the soil was as loose and workable as sand.

"Sugar Babies," Woodrow announced when the field was finally ready for planting. "We'll plant Sugar Babies."

Ellis knew Sugar Babies as small, round melons that tasted honey sweet. He bent and scooped up a handful of the groomed soil. The texture reminded him of oatmeal. "Sugar Babies ought to do just fine," Ellis said.

The melon vines began to sprout in mid-April, lime green buttons cracking through the brown crust of soil. Ellis was amazed by their growth—each day the plants seemed to gain a couple of inches. He would have eaten a bellyful of the rich soil for the same results.

Ellis finished the eleventh grade that spring as the melons grew to the size of baseballs, then softballs, larger and larger. In the surrounding fields of Oak Hills, stalks of tobacco stood knee high. Ellis was hoeing clumps of grass from between the vines one Saturday morning when he saw Benson Bunce's truck roll to a stop in Woodrow's driveway. Woodrow stopped his work and leaned against his hoe as his two brothers walked across the field.

"Hello, Woodrow," Benson said first, smiling and offering his hand. "You got some mighty pretty melons here."

Woodrow engulfed Benson's hand with his own. He nodded in reply.

Porter stepped forward and stuck out his hand. "Yeah, you've been working pretty hard, little brother." He glanced at Ellis. "Who's the kid?"

Ellis swelled out his chest. "My name is Ellis." The brothers had not talked in several months, and now they were awkward and stumbling in their conversation. Ellis busied himself chopping at a tuft of nut grass, but kept his ears open.

"Yeah, a fine-looking field here," Benson said, turning in a semicircle. "Clean as a garden. You've done some work." Benson took a handkerchief from his rear pocket, blew his nose, then studied the contents. He carefully refolded the cloth. "Woodrow," he began, "I know things ain't been right between us lately, and that bothers me. Brothers have to stick together in these times."

Woodrow shrugged. "I ain't mad about nothing."

"Well, we need to stick closer together," Benson continued. "We're Bunces, and no matter what differences we might have, a family is all a man really has."

Woodrow fingered a hole in the bib of his overalls. "We close as we've ever been."

Benson slapped Woodrow's arm. "Shit, Woodrow. I miss having you around. So do Margo and the kids." Benson eyed Ellis, then lowered his voice. "Woodrow. There's a couple of things me and Porter want to talk with you about."

Benson paused to light a Winston. He exhaled the smoke with force, as if relieving his soul of a great burden. "Woodrow, me and Porter need you to ramrod the tobacco crew this year. We've got some outside business interests that are taking up more time than expected. You push the crew—just get them to the fields, keep things going—and this year we'll split the profits three ways."

Benson sucked down another long drag of smoke. "There's another place, Woodrow, where I think we can do some business," he said while exhaling. He leaned and patted one of the melons. "Woodrow, I swear to God, I'm surprised. I didn't think they would grow like this around here. Got me doing some thinking. Porter's done some study, too. You know how down here melons are a dime a dozen after they been on the market a week. It's different up north."

Porter stepped forward. He pushed his glasses up from the end of his nose. "Woodrow, these melons are the earliest maturing that I've seen anywhere. If we were to ship them by truck to produce markets in the north, they'd sell like solid gold. Five, six dollars a melon would be cheap."

"What you say?" Benson cut in. "You know how niggers love

watermelon. Washington is full of niggers. You get these babies out of the field, we'll do the selling and shipping, and we all make a killing."

Woodrow smiled while kneeling on one knee. He cradled one of the young melons in his hands as gently as if it were a human baby. Finally, he shook his head. "No. I wasn't growing these to sell. I ain't messing with tobacco no longer, either."

Porter chuckled meanly. "Shit, Woodrow. What you mean you ain't growing them to sell? The way you've been drawing on your bank account lately, you better be thinking of putting some back."

Woodrow placed the melon back in the crater of soil where it had rested, then stood. "Me and the boy just wanted to grow some melons to see if we could. The money don't matter."

Porter cut his eyes at Benson. "Talk some sense into little brother, will you?"

Benson took his time lighting another cigarette. "Woodrow, I think it's getting time for you to get over this nonsense of yours and come on back home. We can't wait around on you forever. Are you going to run the tobacco crew, or not? Best thing you could do is boot that runt kid back to the Home and get serious about life."

Woodrow shook his head. "Me and the boy will do all right."

Benson squinted as smoke curled around one eye. "You and that boy have about the same amount of sense. You're fucking up, Woodrow."

"Maybe. Least I'm doing it myself."

Ellis could hear Benson and Porter trading curses even as they were getting in the truck to drive away.

"You interested in getting rich?" Woodrow asked, again chopping the earth with his hoe.

"Nope."

"What you interested in?"

"Growing tall enough to punch Benson in his fat nose."

□   □   □

By early June the melons were dark green with white ribs and nearly the size of basketballs. Ellis felt his heart thump one evening when Woodrow took a jackknife from his pocket and cut one of the melons from the vine, rolling the fruit in his hands, feeling the waxy, smooth skin. When he plunged the blade into the melon, Ellis held his breath, heard a crack as the rind split, halves rolling apart to reveal crimson flesh.

Ellis whooped. Woodrow cut a plug from the melon's flesh and handed it to Ellis on the tip of his blade. As Ellis bit in, he tasted a flood of sweet juice.

Woodrow cocked one eyebrow. "Ripe?"

Ellis chewed loudly, nodding vigorously. He spit a seed in an arch. "Sweeter than Kool-Aid."

Woodrow closed the halves of the melon, aligning the edges as if he hoped the wound would heal. He stood, gazing across his lush, four acres. "Boy, you write pretty good?"

Ellis shrugged. "Yeah. I guess so."

"We gonna make us some signs." Woodrow swept his arm before him. "Next weekend is the watermelon feast."

FREE WATERMELON FEAST

AND PIG PICKING

SATURDAY NIGHT AT THE

WOODROW BUNCE PLACE

PUBLIC INVITED

Woodrow and Ellis drove as far as Chapel Hill tacking signs to telephone poles, taping them to store windows, telling people in person.

"We're gonna cook a pig, too," Ellis proudly told the boys of his dorm.

Woodrow was careful to invite everyone who had ever toiled

in the Bunce tobacco fields. He told the pastors of the white and black church congregations to spread the word at Wednesday prayer meeting.

The word spread, no doubt. It circulated at the speed of tongue, which by a law of nature increases in velocity with each telling. Gossip hitched up another notch when word leaked that Woodrow had ordered a couple of kegs of beer. Criticism and enthusiasm for the event contrasted as starkly as biting into the bitter flesh of a green persimmon or into the cool flesh of one of Woodrow's Sugar Babies.

6

adean Tucker puked in the Greyhound's toilet for the fifth time just after the bus left Raleigh. Not much came up, for she had not eaten for days, only a ropey mixture of clear mucus flecked with blood. Her retching was loud, muscle spasms twisting her guts so badly she bit her lip to keep from crying out.

Nadean staggered to her seat, only keeping upright by holding to seat backs. The bus driver frowned at her in the rearview mirror, having already stopped the bus once to see if she was drunk. She huddled in her seat, pressing her forehead against the cool window glass. She sucked in the cold air that flowed from the vents beneath her nose. When the knots twisted again in her belly, she kneaded the scars that tracked up both arms, hoping to squeeze one last molecule of heroin into her veins.

Nadean opened her eyes after the spasm passed. A haze of green foliage rushed past—broad sweet-gum leaves, long pine boughs, fields laid in rows that curved to the forest edge, the brown flash of a tobacco barn.

"Just hold on a little longer," she whispered. "Just a little bit longer."

Nadean spied a child peering at her over the seat top. The little girl stared without blinking, her eyes wide with worry, the only person on the bus not deliberately looking away. A hiss from the mother turned the child's face.

"Hold on, hold on, hold on," Nadean mouthed with each pulse beat that threatened to crack her head.

Only the instinct that drives wounded animals kept Nadean tottering on her feet when she finally stumbled off the bus at the stop in Oak Hills. That instinct had fueled her for the past year while she clung with one hand to a lamp pole, shivering in her short dress. That same instinct would have to carry her one more mile to Mama's house.

For a fraction of a second when Nadean's feet touched home dirt, she remembered with sorrow that four years had passed since she had rolled proudly into Oak Hills, sitting so close to Jerome in his long, bad car. Not a letter home since then. Not a single phone call. Mama must have hurt so bad. Her lament quickly blurred as the world spun; she lurched to the left, stumbled, and went down on one knee. Her dry stomach released nothing but gas when she tried to puke. Through tears, she saw two children standing nearby. They ran when she called to them.

A car squealed to a stop, then backed up. Holding to the branches of a hedge bush, Nadean stood and tried to focus on the face of the woman staring through the window.

"Ma'am, ma'am, you know Essie Tucker?" Sudden cramps made her bend double. The branch snapped and she fell backwards. "Ma'am, could you please take me home," she begged, sprawled on the coarse gravel. "Could you please?"

Nadean heard the car engine roar as the woman accelerated quickly. Across the street, the two children were chattering to a couple of adults. A crowd was gathering.

"She's just drunk" Nadean heard someone say. "We ought to call the law."

"Ain't that one of them Tucker girls?"

Nadean pushed herself to a sitting position. Fine damn homecoming, she thought. No red dress this time, or big car. Just this nasty old skirt—and me sitting here on my ass. The good times gone, girl. They long gone.

"We got a drunk nigger over there," Nadean heard someone shout. Through splintered vision, she saw a figure leave the group and cross the street. The world was spinning again. Nadean remembered the words to a tune: "Get along home, Cindy, Cindy. I'll marry you some day."

Shoot, who gonna marry me now? she wondered. But you still gotta get along home, girl. Nadean fixed one eye on the street. East, out of town. 'Bout a mile. Legs, don't quit me now. She worked herself up to standing.

Nadean took two steps forward, stumbled back three, and went down hard again. She felt gravel cutting into her buttocks. People laughed. The world was a kaleidoscope, slowly drawing to one bright bead. Just before passing out, she felt hands touching her shoulder.

"Mama gonna be so 'shamed of me," she sobbed. "She gonna be so 'shamed."

□   □   □

Mary Stewert slowly pushed her grocery cart through the aisles of Fowler's Grocery Store, past tins of imported teas, fragrant coffee beans, hand-trimmed steaks, and produce only hours from the field. Mary liked quality, and Fowler's represented quality. Damn the higher prices and extra miles she had to drive.

She scanned her shopping list. Capers. Cross and Blackwell, of course. "Excuse me, sir. Can you tell me where the capers are located?"

Mary and Jeffery, her husband, had moved to Oak Hills just two months ago. Their new home was one of the many recently constructed houses in the Whispering Pines subdivision—low eighties in price, cedar siding, decks and skylights, good resale potential; the community was perfect for up-and-coming young professionals.

Yes, here they are, capers. The slender jar clinked against the wire basket. Oriental spices? Oh, I remember where they are. The short rows in the front of the store.

Mary and Jeffery had moved from Connecticut to the Chapel Hill area after Jeffery was hired by a large pharmaceutical firm in the Research Triangle. The new job was a step up, more responsibility, plus a sizable salary increase. Mary had a master's degree in journalism from Columbia and had worked the past two years for a small newspaper in Hartford, but she agreed the move made sense. Jeffery had to climb the ladder while he was still young, while she looked at her writing as an art that could be nurtured slowly. Besides, for the time, she was enjoying being a housewife, while trying to understand this strange culture called the South.

Two young men passed her cart, their arms circling cases of Little Kings beer. Mary chuckled. This culture *was* strange. Life was lived on a binge. Today, Little Kings was the popular beer. Next week, another would take its place. The university's basketball team was idolized to the point of absurdity. Grits came on your breakfast plate in most restaurants even if you didn't order them. Grits—ugh! And, black and white race relations seemed so silly here. Mary had observed that whenever black and white people were together, they flaunted their association, as if shouting, "Look at me. I'm liberal and progressive." So silly. She had never been one to notice color. Mandy was black, had cleaned her mother's house from the time Mary was two until she left for college, and all the while was treated like one of the family. Several black girls had attended her prep school, one graduating with the highest grade-point average. Hadn't she gone to the theater with Tyrone, a medical student she had met at Columbia. She always attended the interracial coffees at the chapel.

But, at least in Chapel Hill, an attempt *was* made. Mary had seen the real South just miles away in Durham where segregation was evident from street to street. Maybe one day she would write a book about the experiences of a Yankee in the South. Maybe she would call the book "Born Again Yankee," or something comical like that.

Mary shopped last for a nice wine. One of the California zinfandels was on sale, so she bought four bottles. She chatted with the young black woman running the register as her groceries were totaled, and was not concerned when the bill was higher than she had estimated. You paid for quality. Besides, for the first time in their marriage, she and Jeffery didn't have to pinch pennies.

Mary spied Woodrow's poster on the bulletin board in front of the grocery store as she was leaving. The crude, red letters stood out boldly beside neatly scribed announcements for yoga classes, notices of rock band performances, and calls for political activism.

A watermelon feast and pig picking? Right in Oak Hills. Woodrow Bunce? Let's see, the Bunces. That name rang a bell. Oh yes, the Bunces are a large farming family. Sort of the aristocracy of Oak Hills.

Mary smiled. She had heard so much about these pig pickings

from Joan and Bob Cheek, how you sat outside and ate barbecued pork and hush puppies with your fingers. All that terrible cholesterol, but it sounded like fun, maybe a chance to meet new neighbors. Something to write about? She knew Jeffery would love to go.

Nadean trembled with fever and ached so badly for three days that when she did rise to consciousness, she wished death would stop her torment. Her sheet was soaked with sweat—vile and pungent—a testimony to the poison she had pumped into her body for years.

Nadean's oldest sister, Jackie, watched her suffering, mopped her forehead with cool cloths, and hourly pulled the sopping bed covers from beneath the frail woman. She sang to her little sister, hugged her when the trembling was worst, and whispered in her ear that she was loved.

Jackie often considered calling an ambulance. Once Nadean had arched her back in spasm and bit her tongue to the blood, and she had rushed her oldest boy out the door to get help. But the spasm had passed, and she had called him back before he reached the mailbox. With no insurance, the hospital had to be life or death. Weren't nothing so new, anyway. Henry Gilmore had returned from Boston in nearly the same condition, and he had lived, though he wasn't much use afterward. Time had to pass, and if a person's heart didn't bust first, the bad stuff would sweat out.

Not many black people were left in Oak Hills. The demise of several small farms had driven most of the younger people into Carrboro or Durham to work. Among the families left, the Tuckers, Smiths, McNairs, the Blues, word spread quickly of Nadean's return. People stopped by the house to leave a bowl of peas, platter of fried chicken, to ask if there was anything they could do. The preacher came each evening to read scripture to Nadean and pray as she rolled and trembled in bed.

Everyone was shocked. Folks found it hard to believe this shivering, bed-pissing creature was Nadean Tucker, the same bright songbird who had last rolled into town riding in that long, white Lincoln. The sheet couldn't hide her hipbones poking sharp as a plow point, her skin pulled tight and pale across her face, mottled like rotten beeswax. Her breasts that had once threatened to split her blouse now barely made the covers rise. And though Jackie tried to keep Nadean covered, so many needle tracks dotted her limbs they were impossible to hide.

People left shaking their heads. The preacher gained enough new material to preach for a month. Mothers hurried to lecture their daughters on the evils of leaving home.

Nadean drifted through stages of sleep. When she broke consciousness, the faces above her swirled with color, splintered, spun, mouths gushing words as hollow as if shouted from the bottom of a deep, deep well.

Who these people, Nadean wondered? What they staring at? She would fall through the mattress again and dream—strange, jumbled dreams of shattered time and places, drifting beneath her eyelids on a quiet, dark pool, sometimes swallowed by bright bubbles floating up from the past.

Sunshine was warm on her face. She was seven. The crushed, green wheat beneath her smelled sweet like milk; a mockingbird chattered from the branches of a gum tree. Nadean blocked the bright sun with her book, smiled at the open page—a palm tree arching like a half rainbow over that blue, blue water. From the book, her eyes flicked to the sky and followed the lazy flight of a single red-tailed hawk. The sky wasn't nearly as blue as that water. *Why I got to live here in ugly old Oak Hills when there places to see like in this book?* The hawk passed on motionless wings, an air current carrying him by as quietly as the moon.

. . . drifting

The Potomac River shone below the bluff in a curving, silver
ribbon. Nadean wondered what shone brightest, the water or the
waxed hood of the long car. Jerome sat close to her, looking so
damn good with that big, fuzzy mustache, that funny way of
squinting one eye when he smiled.

"Me and you, babe, sheee-it. We gonna set this town on fire. It
never be the same again. Way you sing, people gonna fall down
on their knees. Hear me? On their knees."

Nadean felt a shiver of pleasure start at the base of her neck
and run down her spine. She read her name again at the bottom
of the flier advertising Saturday night at the Zodiac Club. She
felt Jerome tighten his hand on her shoulder and knew that life
could never be better than right now. Why couldn't she just
step over the edge of the cliff and sail on that bright ribbon into
heaven?

Nadean tilted her head back and rested it against Jerome's
shoulder. Folks back home—let them stay back home.

. . . drifting

Nadean studied fly specks on the dingy, white ceiling, counted
them, closed her eyes and saw them dotting her eyelids like black
stars. The man moved on top of her, grunting; she felt his soft,
hairy belly rubbing against hers, lifted her arms and circled his
waist, urging him to hurry, then dropped them limp upon the
bare mattress.

. . . drifting

"Now that didn't hurt one little bit, did it, baby?" he asked.
"You know Jerome wouldn't do nothing to hurt you."

No, she had hardly felt the prick of the needle. She was silly to
be so afraid. The dope rushed into her heart, spread through her
arteries, a smooth current pushing her deep into the waterbed. She
closed her eyes to stop the spinning, felt like every breath was an
exhale, opened her eyes to Jerome's sweet face. Suddenly, she felt
sick. Jerome held the wastebasket under her chin, then wiped her
face with a wet rag. Every cell in her body tingled.

"Oh, honey," Nadean whispered. "I feel so good. Soooo very, very good."

. . . drifting

Nadean was singing the chorus of an old hymn she remembered from childhood. She sang low in her throat, her mouth close to the microphone. Beer bottles trembled on tables close to the speaker. Nadean loved everyone in the room; they smiled so sweetly at her through the blue cigarette smoke. She was carrying them home—home to Mama, home to dancing barefoot in the dust on early summer mornings, smelling slab bacon frying slowly, home to those good buttermilk biscuits you could poke a hole in and fill with cane syrup.

Nadean closed her eyes and imagined herself as the little sparrow that used to twitter in the rosebush outside her bedroom window. She could go home that easily, just close her eyes and remember, and sing, and take them all home.

. . . drifting

The lonely coo of a mourning dove. Close. Maybe from one of the pines in the yard. A further dove cooed his answer.

Nadean felt cool air on her forehead. Soft light filtered through her eyelids. It daybreak or twilight? she wondered. Doves don't tell.

Nadean flexed the fingers of one hand. She smelled walls long saturated with coal smoke. Ain't smelled that in a while. I smell collards, too.

She lifted her wrist, then dropped it. Tired, tired, tired, but good tired. Tired like the time I wake up after the scarlet fever. Wrung clean like a washrag. Maybe this just another of the bubbles?

Nadean drew in a long breath. She sucked in the coal odor, her damp hair smelling sweet like well water, heard the wail of another dove. Maybe I dead?

Nadean opened her eyes a crack. Window glass. There dew on

the pane. Must be morning. That clock ticking so loud, sound like the cuckoo Mama had. Where am I?

Nadean heard a creak at bedside and slowly turned her head, her breath catching between heartbeats.

A woman slumped in a rocking chair. Her chin rested against her bosom, the window light striking her hair and casting a shadow across her face—what was the shape of that dark face?

A rooster crowed from nearby. I ain't dead. Nadean felt a tear gather in the corner of her eye.

"Mama," she called softly. "Mama, I'm thirsty."

he smell of slowly cooking pork lapped over Oak Hills, through screen windows, open doors, car windows, reminding people it was time to come to Woodrow's melon field. The day was warm and cloudless, and many people who had given Woodrow's poster only a sidelong glance now found their noses turning in the direction of his house.

A carload of young men arrived first, Harry Crumpler, the Lynch brothers, Jamie Cain, local boys who had bought their school clothes and earned pocket money by working summers in the Bunce tobacco fields. They were already drinking beer and ready for a good time.

"Parr-ty!" Harry shouted as the group walked up the drive.

The black gas cooker stood on four squat legs, smoke rolling from a pipe in the top. Sam Smith, a longtime Bunce field hand, was tending the hog, holding a squeeze bottle of home-concocted barbecue sauce in one hand, a pint of home-brewed corn liquor in the other. Two kegs of Budweiser sat in an old bathtub, surrounded by crushed ice. Fifty of the best melons were cooling in the shade of a willow tree. Woodrow and Ellis stood together, proudly greeting people as they arrived.

A farming couple, Bill and Louise Tate, arrived next. Their three children jumped from the bed of the pickup, followed by a mixed-breed dog. Woodrow's hounds stood against the wire, baying and yelping.

"You right sure he ain't charging by the head?" Louise asked her husband. "You know it ain't like a Bunce to give nothing away."

"Shhhh," he hissed, smiling as Woodrow raised his hand.

Brakes squealed. The activity bus from the Boys' Home pulled onto the shoulder of the road. The dust hadn't settled when both the front and emergency doors flew open and boys piled out, Enzor shouting from the driver's seat, "First one of you I see acting up is going straight home."

Ellis lifted his chin even higher as the boys swarmed across the lawn.

The first blacks to arrive had been Sam's family. They walked in a knot toward the crowd of white people, everyone turning to stare. Although the school had been integrated for years, social events were usually divided down the color line.

Sam, well liquored, shouted for his kin to hurry. "I'm a'cookin' this hog, hear me. I'm cookin' him. Better hurry 'fore there ain't nothing but bones."

By mid-afternoon, more than a hundred white people and a couple dozen blacks were gathered at Woodrow's. In the beginning, folks were polite and stiff, farmers talking crops with other farmers, wives discussing their kids, children and teenagers eyeing one another from scattered, small groups. But Sam passed his pint, beer was swilled, and soon formalities weakened and the fun began. A Frisbee sailed, small children began playing tag, colors and ages began to mingle as if it were just another workday in the fields.

Mary and Jeffery and two other couples from the subdivision arrived. Mary wore a blue, strapless sundress with white sandals, her trim figure and green eyes turning more than a couple of heads. Some of the older people looked upon the newcomers with disdain—Yankee highnoses, not caring a damn for the land and traditions of Oak Hills. After scanning the crowd, Mary walked directly to Woodrow where he stood alone with his arms folded.

"You must be Woodrow Bunce?" Mary asked, thrusting out her hand.

"Yes, ma'am."

Mary laughed. "Oh, stop that 'yes, ma'am' stuff. You'll make me feel old. My name is Mary Stewert and this is Jeffery, my husband. We live just down the street."

Jeffery stepped closer and shook Woodrow's hand. Jeffery was a tall, slender man of twenty-eight, with a boyish face, neatly clipped hair, and dimples. "I'm pleased to meet you, Woodrow." He half turned and pointed across the melon field at a newly built Cape Cod–style house on the edge of the subdivision, less than a hundred yards from Woodrow's front yard. "I guess you would say we're next-door neighbors."

"This is so nice of you to do," Mary cut in. "We've been dying to get to know some of the local people. This is perfect. And I'm happy to see you've invited *everyone.*" Mary glanced at Sam, who was supporting himself by holding to the edge of a picnic table.

Ellis left a group of boys and walked closer to the new woman. He liked the fine hair that gleamed on the curve of her neck, the very white skin that showed above the elastic top of her dress. He liked her speech, faster than people spoke in Oak Hills, sort of nasal, her hands small and delicate, clasped over the swell of her stomach. Bet she ain't never strung tobacco, he mused. Probably never cut a chicken up in her life.

Ellis looked from the woman to her husband, studied his cuffed shorts, Puma sneakers, the little alligator on his shirt. The couple looked similar to the other people from the subdivision— too clean, too starched, not a wrinkle or scuff on them.

Mary and Jeffery and their friends spread blankets on the grass and sat down. Mary took a chilled bottle of Chablis from a straw basket and asked Jeffery to uncork it while she screwed the stems into several plastic goblets. Then she lay out a saucer with a slice of Brie, plus a box of stone-ground wheat crackers.

Woodrow's party was swelling. Many people, who had elected not to come, changed their minds from curiosity. The second keg was tapped. Sam opened the trunk of his car and got out a mason jar filled with white liquor. Teenagers found reasons to wander to the far side of the melon field where they sucked down the harsh smoke from a joint. The sun was hot. Woodrow split a melon with his Case folding knife, dividing it into crimson quarters. He split more melons, people hurrying over to dig into the cool, sweet flesh with their fingers. Hickory smoke spilled from the cooker, contrasting nicely with the perfume of melons, salt of beer, and sting of whiskey. Two men began fighting, but they were too drunk to hurt each other and ended up trading refill trips to the keg. Sam pulled a rib from the hog, held it aloft like a beacon, and shouted, "COME AND GET IT." Church-going people filled their plates and ate so they could leave this miniature Sodom before things got out of hand. After hurrying them through a plate of food, Enzor herded Ellis and the other boys to the bus, every one of them grumbling, smeared with hog

fat and watermelon juice. A fiddle and guitar were tuned by Bill
and Jerry Hicks, brothers who played Saturday nights in a rock-
abilly band. They lit into a lively rendition of "Fox on the Run."
Feet began tapping. A second song followed. The sun hung just
over the treetops. A black couple began buck dancing. A white
couple joined in. Soon, a couple dozen people were hopping and
twirling on the grass.

Jeffery popped a second bottle of Chablis. Mary was slightly
drunk and deep into a philosophical study of southern human
nature. So uptight about color, she thought. Bunched in little
groups, dancing side by side, but never together. Two separate
parties going on at once. She could stand it no longer.

Mary rose from her blanket and set a course for a lone black
man standing at the edge of where people were dancing.

"Will you dance with me?" she asked, taking his hand. The
man balked, then smiled.

Mary mimicked the clogging steps of another woman. Jeffery
lifted his hand in salute. The black man watched Mary's breasts
bounce, shrugged, then broke into his own shuffle.

"Wanna frig?" he asked, leaning close, his breath sweet with
whiskey.

"Oh, no thank you," Mary said gaily. "I'm so full of watermelon, if I ate a fig I would pop right open."

Nadean studied a picture of her mother as a young woman, her jet
black hair, those almond-shaped eyes that made fools out of men,
that trim waist so much like her own. She rocked slowly in the
old oak chair, felt tears again on her cheeks. Been dead a year
now, and I didn't even know it. Didn't know my own mama was
dead. Lord, what kind'a person am I—wouldn't feel it inside
when they own mama die?

From the kitchen came the clammer of pots. Nadean heard steps, and again her sister stood in the doorway.

"We ought to go over there," Jackie said. "Just for a little while. The fresh air do you good. Jim and the younguns been gone an hour."

Nadean didn't answer, just stared at the photo. She wished there was a more recent picture of Essie, for already she found it hard to remember exactly how her mother's face had looked.

"Nothing else, we ought to go so you can say something to Mr. Woodrow," Jackie continued. "Weren't none of them other white people gonna touch you. Let you lay there and die first."

Nadean returned the photo to its shroud of tissue paper, folding the edges neatly and carefully.

Nadean balked at the edge of light circling a large bonfire. Too many people. Too much laughing. Jackie nudged her arm. Nadean smoothed the front of her dress. The garment was a couple sizes too large, but at least would hide some of her skinniness. She fingered her hair, once long to her shoulders and ironed, now mashed under a blue scarf.

"Go on," Jackie whispered. "People be glad to see you."

Nadean entered the fire glow with measured steps, fearing a quick movement, a screech from the fiddle would send her fleeing. She looked beyond everyone's stares.

A few of the black people spoke to her, but their words were short and dripping with politeness. Wide eyes betrayed their attempts to hide their shock, remembering the woman from four years before. They were embarrassed for her now, for they had envied her, bragged on her, hoped—only to have this dope-shooting whore return. Everyone had heard the stories.

Nadean backed against a tree trunk and busied herself in a plate of barbecue and potato salad that Jackie brought her. At least she could eat again. Maybe food still tasted like paper, but it didn't make her retch. Occasionally, she lifted her eyes to find someone staring at her.

Nadean was swallowed up and forgotten by the gaiety. The hog was stripped clean to the bone, bread sopped in the grease, another keg ordered. Old tires were added to the bonfire, the flames leaping twenty feet into the night. Beyond the ring of light, old and new lovers panted, joints were shared, bourbon whiskey and white liquor were belted down. Mary and Jeffery weaved their way from group to group in a crusade to bridge the race gap. It was one hell of a party.

Nadean watched the drunkards, the loud talkers, the dark figures outside the rim of light. She spied Woodrow standing alone, holding a cup of beer. She studied him, that slender smile on his lips, head raised, eyes sweeping over the crowd. He was far from the same Woodrow she remembered from the tobacco fields. Shier than a mud turtle then, kept his eyes on the dirt. Folks had whispered he wasn't right.

Now he stand tall as an oak tree, Nadean observed. Got his head up. Gone and made a big party. He done changed to someone new, like the wintertime slip into spring.

Again Nadean awoke to the sad cry of a mourning dove. The soft light of early morning framed the edges of the shade. Her eyes followed a crack that traced across the plastered ceiling.

Where am I, she wondered? The past couple of years had dulled her panic of awakening in a strange bed.

White stucco ceiling. The walls blue. Sheet smell like a man. Whoever this beside me, he snoring to beat the band. Dove cooing outside? Oh yeah. Oak Hills. I'm back home. Yeah, I been home now a week.

Nadean slowly pivoted her head. Woodrow slept on his stomach, his face toward hers. Air whistled from his nostrils as he breathed.

Nadean studied his face. Not so bad for a white man. Big chin, thick eyelashes, shoulders knotted with muscles, hair all over his chest and growing up his neck. Nadean chuckled. Lord, people 'round here, their tongues would fall out of their mouths if they knew Woodrow Bunce be laying up with a colored girl. His mama would spin in her grave. She thought back to the previous night.

Nadean was ashamed when her sister took her by the hand and led her to Woodrow. His eyes widened when he saw her and Nadean imagined his thoughts—what happened to you, gal? More meat on a chicken neck.

Nadean stared at the ground. "I 'preciate you stopping for me when I was sick, Mr. Bunce, and carrying me to Jackie's house."

Moments of silence. Nadean felt two thick fingers lift her chin. He stared at her, his eyes moving across her cheekbones to her hair, dropping to the razor scar on her chin.

Woodrow did not look with pity. Nadean had seen pity until she was sick of it. Pity was the way most people looked her right in the eyes as if they were afraid to admit they saw the scars, the tight, dry skin, the broken hair. Woodrow looked with the fascination of a child, his eyes studying her face, his finger tracing the scar where the man had cut her. His brown eyes were confused, like a child seeing the bare stalk of a dandelion after blowing the puffball away.

"Let me get you some melons to carry home," he finally said. "I saved some nice ones in the middle of the field."

Woodrow took her hand and led her away from Jackie, the fire, the loud crackle of the drunks.

"I'm sorry 'bout your mama," Woodrow said. Nadean liked his voice, so slow and full and gentle like the wind after a storm has passed. They circled the field, Woodrow pausing to cut two large melons from their vines. A late, waning moon was flooding the treeline. Nadean stumbled twice. When Woodrow asked if she would like to come into his house and rest, she said yes without consideration. She figured she had heard every proposition uttered by man, but never the bait of a rocking chair and cup of hot milk.

Woodrow stirred in his sleep, drawing Nadean's mind back to the present. He coughed.

Bet he be surprised when he wakes up, Nadean thought. First time for him, I know that. Probably give me some money to keep quiet.

She smiled, remembering how the hot milk had made her sleepy, she had nodded a few times, and he had lifted her and carried her to his bed, had wiped her face with a warm cloth.

Let people talk. Talk ain't nothing. It can't hurt me more than I been hurt. Not now.

8

T alk was cheap, and it flowed as rapidly as the beer had at Woodrow's party. The people who stayed to drink the last dregs in the keg swore the party was the best ever held in town, while most of those who stayed home or fled early declared it the worst orgy of drunkenness in the history of Oak Hills.

Few people knew that Nadean Tucker had spent the night with Woodrow. Ellis knew the next morning when he came to help clean up, but told no one out of fear Enzor would find out and stop him from working there. Nadean's sister knew, but after a week of sleepless nights, her emotions wrung dry, the event seemed insignificant. Woodrow was harmless. A few of the late drinkers had noticed Nadean walking with Woodrow, but with next morning's hangovers, wondered if the event wasn't in the league with pink elephants. Picking up women, particularly black women, wasn't Woodrow's style.

Even if the truth had been widely known, the matter would have caused no more than a wagging of tongues had Nadean slipped away early in the morning. More than one farmer had been seen parked at the edge of the woods while carrying home field help. Blue-eyed black children were not uncommon. People gossiped, then forgot. Time healed all but cancer in Oak Hills.

But Nadean didn't slip away from Woodrow's house at daybreak. Two days after she arrived, she and Woodrow finally emerged from the house, drove to the local Piggly-Wiggly, and began buying groceries. They left with a week's supply of food, going next to Marcie Thompson's linen outlet where they bought towels and floral-print bed sheets. Word began circulating.

"It's a sight, ain't it," exclaimed the horrified elderly women of the community. "Law, Amma Bunce would roll in her grave if she knew how her son is carrying on. He was raised right, too. Can't use that excuse." Then in lowered voices, "Course he is soft of mind."

Woodrow and Nadean's shopping spree was spread over several days, buying curtains for the windows, a set of plastic plates and bowls, an iron and ironing board, toilet items, household goods that Woodrow had ignored prior to Nadean. The merchants took his money without raising an eyebrow, then shook their heads in disgust as soon as his back was turned. Woodrow's inheritance had been slight, but in years prior, he had saved all his money and with Porter's advice, had invested in good stock. He was a moderately wealthy man.

"It's sad, that's what it is. You'd think Benson would do something. I know Woodrow can't be held accountable for much of what he does, but things are getting out of hand."

Many of the younger men in Oak Hills, especially those who had worked in the Bunce fields, shared a more tolerant opinion.

"That damn Woodrow, can you believe it? What's that crazy fucker going to do next? Got him a little 'pigger nussy' and went hog wild."

The black community of Oak Hills avoided the topic. Nadean had already disappointed them so much, she was best forgotten.

Benson Bunce was soon aware of the actions of his younger brother. At the end of the week, when it was evident that Woodrow was not just on a fling, he and Porter again drove to Woodrow's house.

Woodrow met his brothers on the front porch. Nadean, remembering Benson's temper, stood listening with dread from inside the front door.

The older brothers didn't bother starting with small talk. "Woodrow, there's some bad gossip going around that needs settling today," Benson began.

Nadean peered through a part in the curtains. Woodrow nodded once at his brothers. "I'm listening."

"Yeah," Benson answered. "You're listening? Well, good. About damn time. What's this shit about you shacking up with that Tucker girl?"

Woodrow hooked his thumbs over his back pockets. He shrugged. "Ain't much to it."

"Ain't much to it?" Benson glanced at Porter. "Folks tell me you've been walking around like you're in some kind of cloud. Acting strange."

"Spending a hell of a lot of money, too," Porter added.

Benson squinted one eye as he studied Woodrow's face. Woodrow looked down, shuffled his feet. "You been taking your medicine?" Benson asked.

Woodrow violently shook his head. "It ain't . . . it ain't that!" he stammered.

"It's not?" Benson asked. "You sure? If it ain't craziness,

brother, what are you trying to pull? Shacking up with some God damn nigger whore. That ain't craziness?"

Nadean felt a shaft of pain run between her temples. She pressed her forehead against the window glass. Porter lay his hand on Benson's shoulder and hushed him.

"You shh . . . you shouldn't say that, Benson. I'm a grown man now."

Porter nodded in agreement. "We're going to talk this over like men. Like brothers," Porter said. He stepped closer to Woodrow. Woodrow took his thumbs from his pockets, letting his arms hang straight.

"Woodrow," Porter began. "You're a Bunce. There's no prouder name in this county. Hell, there ain't nothing wrong with you having a little fling. Happens to all of us. But, now ain't it about time to straighten up? Huh? People are starting to talk."

Porter nodded at Benson, who then sighed. "All right, maybe you're just having a little fun. Ain't nothing wrong with that. I've had mine. But now, it's time to start acting with some sense again."

"But, I just want to live on my own. Have a place of my own like most people." Woodrow stiffened his arms against his sides, his eyes flicking from the porch to Benson's face, his shoulders slumped.

"There's plenty of room in the big house," Porter said. "Enough of this shit. The tobacco is nearly ready to barn. Like we told you weeks ago, you run the crew and we'll split three ways."

Benson rapped the porch railing with his knuckles. "Woodrow, I can see you wanting your own place. Hell, that ain't no problem. We can have this house jacked up and moved to the farm in a week's time. Put it under some of the oaks where it's cool. You'll have the whole farm for your yard. That damn subdivision is swallowing this place clear up."

"But I like having something that is just mine."

Porter slapped Woodrow's shoulder. "You know it would kill
Ma over again if she knew how you're living, Woodrow. She
always did worry over you twice as much as the rest of us. What
you think Dad would say if he was still alive? Come on, what
you say? Let's give that nigger a few dollars and put her on the
next bus back to Washington. You come on home."

Through her peephole, Nadean saw Woodrow slump, standing round-shouldered like she remembered from old days. He
wouldn't look his brothers in the face. She ached at the memory
of the giant who had lifted her like a pillow and carried her to
rest in his bed. Thought he was filled with iron. A tree. Now him
shrinking like a busted balloon.

A June bug buzzed across the porch, crashed into the screen,
and fell to the floor. The insect lay on its back, legs churning,
spinning slowly in a circle. Nadean saw Woodrow move his eyes
from the toes of his boots to the helpless bug. Porter extended his
foot and crushed it.

The slaughter of the insect must have touched some emotion
deep inside of Woodrow, for Nadean saw his shoulders slowly
rise till they were square again, his head lift, jaw thrust forward,
his back straighten like an oak beam. Woodrow moved his eyes.
He looked first into Porter's face, then at Benson. "I'm staying
here. She's welcome to stay with me as long as she wants."

Porter's hand trembled as he lit a cigarette. Benson slapped the
porch railing and turned to face the road. "We've warned you,
Woodrow," Porter said. "You're not acting rational. Don't think
for a minute we're going to stand around and let you dirty the
family name."

Woodrow stood in the center of his porch watching as his
brothers drove away. Nadean came from the house and rested her
forehead against the space between his shoulder blades.

□   □   □

Through bits of conversation with the cleaning girl who came twice a week, Mary Stewert learned of the controversy surrounding Woodrow. That evening over dinner, she told Jeffery.

"Basically, the problem is that the bedrock of Oak Hills can't tolerate the idea of a racially mixed couple living here."

Jeffery twirled a strand of fettuccine around his fork. "Baby, you don't make waves in these small, southern communities. Remember what happened in *Easy Rider?*"

"Jeffery, that was a movie, and this is 1983. I feel like climbing on top of the roof and shouting, 'Hey, you crazy bunch of rednecks, wake up!' The Civil War has been over for more than a century." Mary recalled the many hours she had spent working as a volunteer for the "One World" campus committee.

Click went Jeffery's fork against the china. He reached for the bottle of zinfandel. "Eat."

"I can't eat. This whole situation is like out of a play. It's so ridiculous."

"What do you know about this Woodrow character, anyway?"

"I know enough to like him. Don't you?"

Jeffery lifted one shoulder, then dropped it. He swilled a half glass of wine. "Yeah, what I know of him."

Mary recalled the snatches of conversation she had been able to get out of the mousy young cleaning girl. "From what I gather from talking with Alice, Woodrow has always been the town eccentric, a free spirit. He strikes me as a holdout from the sixties. The lady living with him is Nadean Tucker, and from Washington. Alice said she was in entertainment, I don't know, maybe the theater. Both sound like interesting people to get to know better."

Jeffery speared a stalk of steamed broccoli. He nibbled at the seed head, then added a squeeze of lemon juice. "Well, from what I've observed of Oak Hills in two months, this is one of those typical little communities desperately trying to hang on to its small-town atmosphere. To a lot of people, it's important to keep life the way they are accustomed to it."

"I can understand that. To a point. But, Jeffery, I feel it is just as important for people like us to support Woodrow, to support change. We're educated. We've traveled. These people need to learn there is no one set of standards that should rule the world."

Mary sighed, then began nibbling at her food. The pasta was cold. An idea suddenly flooded her mind that caused the corners of her mouth to rise.

"I've got it. Why don't we host a dinner party for Woodrow and Nadean? Sort of return the favor. We can have a cookout, something simple, invite a few friends, and at the same time, let Woodrow see there are at least a few liberal people in Oak Hills."

Jeffery cut his last strand of pasta into short pieces, then stacked them on the tines of his fork. "Sounds fine to me. Who would we invite?"

"Oh, that's easy. Paul and Linda would just eat this up, and so would Tom and Pam. Dack and Shelby were at Woodrow's barbecue and loved it."

Mary's eyes sparkled. She gestured as she talked. "We could grill some nice salmon steaks, make a salad. Shelby went to school at George Washington, so she and Nadean should hit it off. I've been dying to talk with Woodrow about the history of Oak Hills. At the very least, they will see there are a few people in this community with progressive minds."

Jeffery shrugged. He coped with life with a shrug. "Raise hell, babe."

Two weeks had passed since the watermelon feast, and the sun still rose daily over Oak Hills. The gossip concerning Woodrow and Nadean continued to grow like a bushfire and overshadowed the news that Larry Mercer's fifteen year old daughter was pregnant.

Finally, Nadean could stomach the smell of pork frying. She slept her first night through without crying out from a bad dream. She also began to fight the voice that urged her into Woodrow's house that first night.

"Get what you can from this white man," the voice had whispered. "He foolish as they say, you can skin him clean."

Nadean listened. After so many years of living on her wits, she knew to take whatever favors came her way and store them for the bad times sure to follow.

Oh, I'll just check him out a couple of days, Nadean decided that second morning when Woodrow suggested they go buy groceries. She found his poker face soothing after so many people staring at her under furrowed brows. Sister be glad to get rid of me, anyhow. I'll just hang around here a couple of days till I rested, then move on. This Woodrow like a big puppy. Ain't never seen no ass before. I liable to come out of here with a load of money.

Nadean felt long-numbed emotions begin to stir her heart, the afternoon Woodrow defended her against his brothers. Until then, she had looked at their relationship as even. Woodrow supplied food and a bed. She filled the bed. As she watched Woodrow shrink under the barrage from his brothers, she had been seconds away from heading for the bedroom and slipping that hundred dollars lying on the dresser into her pocket, and sliding out the back door. But in that last moment, he turned strong again, and she had felt emotions—couldn't even name them now—but instantly felt shame over thinking of stealing from a man angered by the death of a June bug.

Riding into Chapel Hill with Woodrow—Nadean humming. Can't remember the last time I felt so good. Buy me some new clothes, throw Jackie's old rags away. Woodrow got his pocket full of money.

Inside the shop, Nadean wandered the aisles between racks of new blouses and skirts. She pressed bunches of fabric against her nose, the smell better than flowers. How long it been since I had new clothes?

Nadean discovered her dress size had shrunk by two numbers. Finally, she found a red dress that fit, several blouses and skirts. Woodrow followed her from rack to rack, nodding at clothes she held up. Nadean felt as giggly as the coeds that frequented the store.

Back at Woodrow's, Nadean stood for minutes over the clothes, trying to decide what to wear. Finally, she lay the red dress over the back of a chair and went to bathe.

Nadean powdered her body before slipping on new under-things and then the dress. For the first time, she thought she might actually enjoy the feel of Woodrow's arms around her. The dress was a bit large, but the belt gathered the material in folds that helped hide her skinny hips. She carefully brushed her hair while peering into the hand mirror Woodrow used to shave. Nadean felt silly over her pampering when she walked from the bedroom. He probably wouldn't even notice she was dressed up. "Woodrow," she called. He turned. For a moment, Nadean thought the clouds that forever dimmed his eyes parted, and he looked at her with a focus that was new. He only nodded, but with the movement of his head, Nadean felt more appreciation than in a hundred catcalls. She lifted the hem of her dress and twirled.

"Ain't I pretty, Woodrow? Red as one of them cardinals hopping 'round the yard."

Nadean tried to see her full reflection in the window glass, but her image was distorted. "Man, ain't you got a mirror here bigger than that little thing you shave with?" she complained.

Woodrow shook his head.

"Lord, Woodrow, you scared your face will break a big mirror? Why don't you have a big mirror hanging on the wall?"

Woodrow pushed out his lip in thought. He brushed back a lock of hair that hung over one brow. "I ain't never spent much time examining myself."

Woodrow's simple words, slapped against Nadean's ears as if he had clapped his hands . . . Ain't never spent much time examining myself. Nadean heard the sentence even as she lay in bed that night. She could remember few days in her life that she hadn't stood before a wall mirror. She remembered studying her reflection after the first time with "uncle," wondering if the glass reflected her shame, Sunday mornings spending ten minutes moving a rose from one shoulder to the other, trying to decide where it looked best, gazing at herself wishing her skin were white, her hair straight and golden, wishing the next hour her skin were as black as the ebony African princess in the picture book. If she had ever worshiped anyone or anything, the icon had been her own reflection.

Woodrow, she thought, staring at the trickle of moonlight through the window. Listen to him sleeping. Ain't worried 'bout nothing. People think he crazy 'cause he don't give a nickel for a mirror. The man knows his face the same, day to day.

As the mourning doves began to call up the sun, Nadean knew she wanted to stay with Woodrow, at least long enough to learn the secret of a life without mirrors.

Mary Stewert walked with determined strides up the drive leading to Woodrow's porch. She glanced at the twin, cane-back rocking chairs, the footstool, pressed her bangs into place, and knocked on the front door. She heard the scrape of chair legs, then long heavy steps. Woodrow opened the door and stood towering over her, blinking at the bright afternoon light.

"Hello, Woodrow," Mary said, extending her hand. "I don't know if you remember me or not, but my husband and I attended your barbecue."

Mary smiled, then took a deep breath to quiet her racing heart. God, I'll be embarrassed if he doesn't remember me, she thought.

Woodrow tugged his earlobe, narrowed one eye. Sunlight was on his face, and Mary was surprised by the deep gray of his eyes, like lake water beneath a storm. She had the sudden uncomfortable feeling that he stared through and beyond her.

"You live over yonder," Woodrow said, lifting his arm and pointing toward the subdivision.

"That's right," Mary said with relief. "On Mockingbird Lane." She heard more footsteps approaching the door. Mary was shocked at the appearance of the frail woman, so gaunt she appeared to be recovering from an illness.

"You must be Nadean?" Mary exclaimed, holding out her hand. "I'm one of your neighbors, Mary Stewart." As they shook hands, Mary noticed the long stare the thin woman gave her pear-shaped diamond.

Nadean lifted her eyes, smiled. Woodrow stared above Mary's head toward the horizon. Several seconds of silence followed. "Won't you come in?" Nadean offered.

"Oh, no," Mary said. "I was just popping by. I, ah, heard you were living here, Nadean, and just wanted to invite the two of you to a cookout at my house this Saturday evening. I have several friends who would like to meet you, and besides, we *are* practically next-door neighbors."

Mary felt her heart thump again when Nadean looked up at Woodrow.

"Nothing fancy," Mary continued. "Just a few couples so things will be comfy."

Nadean raised one eyebrow at Woodrow. Woodrow continued staring at the horizon until Nadean nudged his arm. "You want to go to a cookout, Woodrow?"

Woodrow turned his head toward Mary and blinked, as if he had forgotten she stood there. "You need a hog?"

Mary chuckled. "Oh, no. I wouldn't even attempt to try to match your barbecue. I was thinking of grilling salmon."

More seconds of quiet. "You want to go eat?" Nadean asked, her voice tight and high.

Woodrow lifted his shoulders, then dropped them. "What time?"

Triumph. Mary's bosom swelled with confidence. "Well, *wonder-ful*. Is sevenish all right?"

Woodrow nodded. Nadean smiled, then lowered her eyes. "We bring something?"

"Just yourselves and an appetite. Oh, and everything will be *very* casual."

"Sevenish," Woodrow echoed, trying out the sound. "Casual."

Mary planned the cookout with unusual care. A couple of stressful hours were spent deciding who to invite. Mary knew how important it was to have the right chemistry among guests. She added names to a list, scratched some off, added others, matching and cross matching personalities and professions.

"Woodrow seems like the type who would be comfortable in any crowd," Mary told Jeffery. "He has such a calm presence. But Nadean, she's very interesting, delicate, almost fragile. I wonder if she's into modern dance?"

Finally, three couples were invited. Everyone accepted the invitation with enthusiasm. Now, to prepare the right menu.

Butterflies churned in Nadean's stomach while dressing for dinner Saturday afternoon. Although she was firm in her resolve to live in a world minus mirrors, she could not help sneaking a few peeks into Woodrow's hand glass.

Fancy-dressed white woman, she complained. Toting a diamond on her finger big as a bird egg. Ain't gonna know a soul. What somebody like me say to them people? What they know 'bout me?

Nadean tried on all her clothes, finally deciding on a yellow skirt and long-sleeved blouse to hide the needle scars on her arms. Around her neck she placed a necklace made of red and blue cut glass. Last, and feeling guilt at her weakness, she put on a little powder and lipstick from the cosmetics she had stowed at the back of the dresser drawer.

Sevenish to Woodrow meant seven on the dot. Casual was a clean pair of his overalls, and a flannel shirt with the sleeves rolled up to his elbows. He and Nadean climbed the Stewerts' front steps with thirty seconds to spare.

Nadean patted her hair into place. "We gonna stay long?" she asked.

"Long enough to eat," Woodrow answered.

Nadean was glad she had sneaked some makeup when Mary answered the door, wearing a white silk blouse and pearls. That casual, I'm a Jew, Nadean thought. She and Woodrow were kissed on the cheek, then ushered through the house to the patio. Nadean marveled at the lush interior: soft stuffed furniture, a huge fish tank, track lighting, rugs scattered on the hardwood floor, a stereo that filled half a bookcase built into a wall.

Jeffery was pouring wine as they approached. He kissed Nadean and shook Woodrow's hand before giving each a crystal goblet. "I'm very glad you could come. Hope you like Margaux '82."

Nadean grasped the stem of her glass so tightly her fingers ached. She took a quick swallow, clicking the fragile rim against her front teeth. She was glad the stereo was playing. She nervously fingered her large beads, then noticed Mary staring at

them. "Ain't these pretty," she blurted. "Woodrow got these for
me at a yard sale."

Mary nodded quickly. "Oh, they are so—so colorful."

Nadean smiled happily in agreement, then rested her hand on
Woodrow's arm.

The other guests arrived in a group at ten past the hour—all
professionals, registered Democrats, and vanguards of the new
invasion of the South. They smiled while being introduced to
Woodrow and Nadean, graciously accepted a glass of wine, and
settled into a ring of patio chairs. Nadean rested one hand against
the side of her goblet to keep it from shaking. She knew she was
again deep inside the world of mirrors. They mighty bright birds,
she thought. Why they get so dressed up just to come and see me
and Woodrow? Maybe they just poking fun? She tugged down
the cuffs of her blouse.

Woodrow sniffed the rim of his goblet, stared at the red wine,
then lifted the glass and drank it to the bottom. He held the last
half swallow in his mouth, swishing it over his tongue and gums,
shuddering slightly over the bitter taste. Immediately, Jeffery offered a refill, but Woodrow said no. Nadean felt a slight loosening of the tentacle of fear binding her heart.

Circles of small talk.

"Isn't it terrible how the wildlife department is doing nothing
to keep motorboats away from the bald eagle nesting areas on
Jordan Lake?" Tom asked. "I'm afraid every eagle there will leave
if something isn't done soon."

"Well, I think power boats should be banned from the entire
lake," Shelby answered. "All that horrible noise they make and
fumes, not to mention the wake. Dack and I have sailed the Hobie
right past eagles without disturbing a single one."

Jeffery uncorked a second bottle of wine. "Well, do you really
think that a government that supports terrorism in Central America gives a damn about the nesting habits of bald eagles?"

A round of laughter. The conversation swung to the Middle East. Sue leaned close to Nadean and whispered, "I understand you were an entertainer in Washington?"

Nadean felt her heart freeze, then thump like a trapped animal. Her face began to burn. "I sing a little," she whispered.

"Really? Oh, I've always envied people who can sing. I can't carry a tune in a bucket. Would you consider coming and performing at the Ninth Street Bakery?"

"Where's that?"

Sue turned to Paul. "Paul. Nadean is a singer. Wouldn't it be wonderful if she would perform at the Bakery?"

Without waiting for an answer, Sue turned back to Nadean. "You'll have to come with us sometime. The Bakery is the most quaint little place in Durham. Like something out of the Village."

A question from Dack. "Nadean, give us your thoughts. You lived in Washington for a long time, didn't you?"

Nod . . . Nadean's throat drawing tight with panic.

"Doesn't it look ridiculous to see all those fine government buildings and museums surrounded by some of the most desperate poverty in this country?"

Nadean searched for something to say, stammered on her first word, but was rescued by Mary.

"Oh, Dack, don't get Nadean depressed by talking about poverty. Of course it looks ridiculous."

Nadean relaxed against the back of her chair and breathed again. These people do more talking than looking, she thought. You talk about something long enough, it starts looking that way.

The conversation turned. Nadean suffered through another half hour of mindless small talk before a realization began in a quiet corner of her brain. She urged it forward.

"Woodrow," Paul asked, "you're certainly not what I would

call the run-of-the-mill farmer. You seem pretty innovative. Don't you feel that many of those huge midwestern farmers have brought their financial problems on themselves by getting greedy?" Paul didn't wait for an answer. "It seems to me that many of these farmers were pretty silly to . . ."

While listening to Paul, Nadean was able to nudge her bubble of realization forward enough to put it into words. These people don't see you, girl. They don't see you or Woodrow no more than they see them damn eagles on the lake. All they see is what they want to see.

Nadean finished her wine. She felt the beginning of a giddiness that could not all be blamed on the alcohol. These people see the real me 'bout as much as any of the johns ever saw me. Men gave me money to dress like a little girl, put on some leather, pee in some of them's faces, whatever their turn-on be. These folks here the same way.

Nadean slowly relaxed. She accepted a second glass of wine, uncrossed her legs, and leaned back. Seems they already got me figured out. I better not disappoint them. What my Ph.D. in?

Nadean began answering up to questions, even made a few comments on her own. She found her voice taking on volume, as she became not just a performer, but an activist and liberated woman.

"They ought to keep all the boats away from the eagles," Nadean offered. "If somebody wants to see the eagles, let him swim out there."

Paul nodded, sticking out his bottom lip. "So, what you're saying, Nadean, is that the nesting area should be made into a wildlife refuge?"

"Better still," Nadean continued, "keep every damn body away. Let the eagles be eagles. Folks want to see an eagle, look in a book."

Eyebrows were raised at the suggestion. Nadean knew she was on a roll. "The eagle ain't gonna disappear if people ain't staring and counting. People quit watching so close, the eagle can get on with his business, and folks can pay more attention to their own selves."

Woodrow smiled. The other guests wore masks of deep thought. Nadean wanted to laugh. She sensed they saw beyond her, way past to a woman who was an expert on eagles and ecology.

Everything gets turned backwards when you look at life in a mirror, Nadean realized. Folks see things turned around, see it from the wrong side. They don't see the real you. Like Woodrow. Ain't one soul in this town seen him as he really is all his life.

The conversation changed and interchanged. Nadean the naturalist and Woodrow the maverick farmer listened and occasionally commented on what they had observed of the world, and felt slightly drunk and thoroughly hungry when Mary announced that dinner was ready.

These people really putting on the dog, Nadean thought while taking her chair. Table all covered with that pretty laced cloth. Got enough plates and glasses and forks to feed half the town. What the hell that skinny fork for?

For hors d'oeuvres, Mary served mushrooms stuffed with crabmeat and spinach. A white wine was uncorked. The guests waited with their cloth napkins in their laps until Mary was seated. Nadean felt her confidence ebbing. She could bullshit with the best of them, but good table manners were hard to fake.

Mary passed the full bottle of wine to Woodrow. He studied the label, then looked over the three glasses that formed a halo above his plate. Woodrow lifted his full water glass, twisted in his chair, and tossed the water and ice in a holly bush. "Ain't no sense in messing up a clean glass," he explained.

Boosted by Woodrow, Nadean forgot mirrors again. When the bottle came to her, she decided to be the first to fill the long, slender glass. "Beautiful bouquet," she announced, mimicking what she had heard earlier.

"You really know your wines," Mary said, pleased at her selection.

Thick, grilled salmon steaks. Baked potatoes and fresh, steamed asparagus. Champagne was served with the cheesecake. Nadean hoped her stomach wouldn't bust. Woodrow stifled a belch with one hand. Mary began circulating cups of rich-smelling coffee.

Nadean hated to mess up a good high by pouring coffee on top of it, and thought of asking for another glass of bubbly champagne. But she accepted a cup, making herself remember how prolonging the good times had come very close to killing her. She settled back in the chair and listened as the alcohol-inspired conversation probed new areas: Lebanon, American imperialism, the dangers of a rising tide of conservatism and the need for liberal opposition, the American poor.

"What do you think is the best way to combat hunger?" Woodrow was asked.

"Share," he spit out between mouthfuls of cheesecake.

Mary smiled and thought back to the watermelon feast, the image of Woodrow splitting the melons and handing pieces to anyone holding out an arm. She liked his logic—simple and wise.

Too much food and wine had been consumed for the Trivial Pursuit game to be taken seriously. Finally, Jeffery pulled cards at random and read them to be answered at grabs. Nadean was pleased to discover she knew the answers to several questions concerning music and movies. Eleven o'clock chimed on the cuckoo clock. Woodrow stood, stretched, and announced he had to go home.

Round of handshakes. Promises to get together. "We enjoyed so much having the two of you over," Mary said at the front door.

"We enjoyed it, too," Nadean answered. She gritted her teeth to kill a yawn.

"Let's get together soon," Jeffery said. "Maybe we could go out one night for a drink."

"And Woodrow, Nadean," Mary said in a hushed, throaty voice. "I just want you to know that every one of us here tonight is behind your relationship all the way. Remember that."

Jeffery uncorked a bottle of brandy for a nightcap when he and Mary returned to the circle.

"Aren't they delightful," Mary said. "So spontaneous and different. But, those beads Nadean was wearing! I'm sure she meant them as a joke."

"Philosophical is the very definition of Woodrow," Sue said. "I love the way he pauses to think everytime before he speaks. More people should do that. And I'm mesmerized by how he stares off into the dark like he sees things no one else does."

"I like Nadean," Dack said. "Not a pretense to her. And what a sense of humor."

Mary poured a half glass of brandy. She twirled the liquor, letting a little bit slip over the rim of the glass. "We'll straighten this community out yet," she announced. "Little by little by little."

Woodrow and Nadean slowly walked the quarter mile home. The musty sweetness of decaying melons filled the air.

"They nice people," Nadean said, "but you ever see anyone so upset over things? I lived as nice as they do, I wouldn't give a damn 'bout no birds."

"What birds?" Woodrow asked.

ummer in Oak Hills passed slowly under evening thunderstorms, heat, the lazy buzz of seven-year locust. Woodrow and Nadean's affair continued to lead the rounds of local gossip. The members of the white Methodist church held a special prayer meeting in hopes that Woodrow would be shown the ways of his sins. Benson and Porter went so far as going to talk to a judge about having Woodrow committed against his will, but were told that as long as he was not a threat to himself or society, he could do as he pleased.

But as the heat of August descended, the major shock passed

and talk began to die out. Other happenings took center stage. William Carter's second-oldest boy was killed when he split his car in half against a hickory tree. Rumor had it he had been drinking. Gossip surrounded the arrest of the mayor's son for misdemeanor possession of marijuana.

Cool mornings in late September signaled the death rattle of dog days. Woodrow and Nadean and Ellis plowed the melon field and planted a quarter acre in collards and mustard greens. Slowly, Nadean gained weight.

Woodrow's few acres were now an island, surrounded on all sides by the expanding subdivision. Daily, more prime farming land and forest were rent by bulldozer. The ringing of twenty-four-ounce framing hammers drowned out the chatter of busy squirrels, the flutter of southbound birds.

Woodrow and Nadean became a cause célèbre to many residents of the subdivision. They were invited to several more dinners and parties, as everyone seemed to want to become acquainted with this pioneering couple of the new South.

Nadean learned to enjoy the attention. It helped repair an ego that had seen the hard, lonely bottom. And she felt safe, for she realized she was only a reflection to these people, a mirror image of their own values and opinions. Her hosts saw only the wine and words they filled her with, the intoxicant needed that night for them to feel worldly and conscientious. Nadean learned to answer questions according to how she felt, and to lower her head and decline comment whenever something revealing was asked. They were too polite to probe.

Woodrow came for the cooking. Each dinner seemed in competition to best the previous host. He ate the fancy food with a meat-and-potatoes approach, answered questions in his usual few words, unintentionally adding to his reputation as a man of thought. The array of silver that had cluttered Mary's table gradually dwindled to a spoon, knife, and fork. China was replaced by earthenware. Woodrow's style became a fad.

Sometimes when mellowed by wine, a question would snap Nadean's memory back to the reality of Washington, back to the Zodiac Club, and for a second, just a second, she longed for those good times before the needle, the bright lights of the clubs, the deep bass chords of jazz. But just as quickly, the terrible memories of her last year in Washington overpowered the snatches of good, and she was happy to be home in Oak Hills—happy she had been able to return to the same peaceful site of her youth.

Nadean turned thirty the first Tuesday in October. Her sister stopped by briefly to leave her a cake and tell her they were moving into a new housing project in Durham.

"I didn't know it was your birthday," Woodrow apologized after Jackie left.

"I didn't tell you it was my birthday, neither. Ain't nothing to a birthday."

"I want to get you something. Want a new dress?"

"Woodrow, I got me clothes to last ten years."

"Well, there's got to be something you want. You ain't much older than a youngun, and younguns want everything."

Nadean laughed. "Woodrow, I'm so far from a youngun, it ain't funny. But, you get me started thinking like a youngun, I could write you a book on what I want."

"Tell me something."

Nadean stared toward the ceiling. "Oh, I like to be president. Be able to fly. Be a boy for a day. Have a pony."

Nadean remembered a picture book she had loved as a child. The book contained pictures of pretty places in America: high mountains, beaches, tall city buildings, deserts. The pages were dog-eared and soiled, the cover ripped off. She had loved the book better than her dolls.

Her favorite picture was a beach in Florida, white sand piled like sugar beside lapping blue water, coconut palms curving against a clear sky. In the shallow water stood several pink birds resting on one leg. Nadean smiled. She had always been drawn to that picture, so distant from any tobacco fields, no smelly outhouse in sight or pan of butter beans to shell. She knew she could lie in that warm sand and sleep and sleep.

"I'd like to have my own beach," she whispered, her mind still in Florida. "Lay in the white sand. I get a little hot, just jump in the water and cool off. Crack me a coconut if I get hungry." She giggled. "That's what the youngun in me would want most, Woodrow. But the youngun in me is gone. I got the things I need now."

Woodrow grunted and nodded. He lifted his hand and sucked on the tip of his thumb. "Dig a pool," he finally said. "That ain't no beach, but I could haul in some sand. Make it look like a beach." Woodrow stared at the wall, deep into his thoughts. "I never did learn to swim."

Nadean laughed again, noting the deep think lines crossing Woodrow's forehead. "You gonna grow me some palm trees, too? Lord, you know how to grow everything else."

"Don't know much about palm trees," he answered. "Reckon they grow 'bout like other things."

Nadean had come to realize that whenever Woodrow stared, he was seeing things very real and serious. She reached across the table and rested her hand on top of his.

"You're one sweet man, Woodrow. A sweet and crazy, crazy man."

Billy Williams was the tallest boy in the senior high dorm at the Home. He had lived in the Home for five years, since his mother ran off while his father was away on another trip with the merchant marines. He was stockily built, loud-mouthed, and a bully.

Billy's father had visited him just once in five years, but he did write monthly, prompting the boy to parade up and down the floor, bragging of where his father was now, how rich he was becoming, and how, very soon, he was coming to take him away.

Earlier in the afternoon, Billy had received another letter, this one postmarked in Japan.

"Dad says he'll be home in three months, and then we're going to buy a farm down in Florida and grow oranges. Says we'll be partners."

Each letter seemed to carry a different proposal, though none had ever materialized. Few of the boys believed the stories, many wondering if Billy made them up.

"I'm gonna eat oranges till green branches are sticking out my ass," Billy bragged. "You suckers will still be here till old man Enzor kicks you out."

Ellis was lying on his bunk, counting his money and feeling angry. Since Nadean's arrival, he had only worked for Woodrow a couple days a week. He was jealous of Nadean, but stowed that emotion in the same far chamber where he kept other griefs and disappointments.

"Hey, runt," Billy called. "In a year, I'll have more money in my pocket than you'll see the rest of your life."

Ellis lifted his eyes from the stack of bills. "You even know where Japan is?"

"Hell, yeah."

"Where?"

"Since when do I have to answer your questions?"

Ellis began stuffing his money back into the sock. "Japan is a long way from here. On the other side of the earth."

"So what?"

"So, I doubt your old man is really serious about growing oranges."

Billy smirked. "What the hell do you know? You got an old man, runt? You ever get letters?"

Ellis felt a blush burn under his eyes. "No, I don't get letters." He swung his feet off the mattress. "But I don't get a bunch of hogwash neither."

Billy started toward Ellis. "You calling my dad a liar? You calling him a liar, runt?"

Hobbies and homework stopped. Fights took top billing. Except for a boy guarding the door, everyone in the dorm ringed the young combatants.

"You take that back and say you're sorry," the larger boy warned, "else you'll be swallowing your teeth in about one minute."

"Fuck you," Ellis answered. He was scared, but kept his chin lifted, his fists balled by his side. He bit his lip to keep it from trembling. He had finally begun to grow, but was still no match for Billy.

Billy grinned. "Pygmy here must think he's grown about two feet overnight. Hey fellas, don't you think I ought to stomp his runt ass?"

"Yeah, kick his little butt."

"I wouldn't let him say that about my dad."

Billy jabbed Ellis's chest with his finger. "You gonna apologize, pygmy? My patience is running out."

Ellis could feel his pulse in his temples, and his throat was dry. He had fought Billy twice in the past and been beaten badly. He tried to swallow. Die before I'll back down, he thought.

"One last chance, pygmy. Say you're sorry good and loud."

Ellis studied the way Billy stood, cocky, his legs planted wide and his hands on his hips. Ellis shifted his weight to his left leg.

Having grown so large so young had slowed Billy's reflexes, and when he dropped his hands and swung a wide haymaker, Ellis slipped it, and kicked upward. His foot rammed into Billy's crotch. Billy gasped, grabbed his belly, and bent double. Twice, Ellis jabbed the larger boy's head as the fellows screamed.

Billy straightened up after the blows to his head, then lashed out a right that backed Ellis up. Soon, he had the smaller boy on the floor, battering his stomach and chest.

"Kick me in the nuts will you, you little cocksucker," Billy shouted. "You'll pay for it."

Ellis covered his groin with one hand, pounding Billy's ribs with the other. Billy could punch harder, and just when Ellis feared he might start crying, the guard began shouting.

"Enzor's coming! Enzor!"

The boys raced to their bunks. Billy socked Ellis once more in his gut, then leaped up and ran. Ellis had just climbed to one knee when the door burst open. He shuffled to his bunk and flopped down.

"What's all the noise in here?" Enzor shouted. He started toward Ellis. "What's the matter with you, McDonald?" He twisted Ellis around to face him. "You been fighting again?"

Enzor searched up and down the dorm. Billy hid his face behind a book.

"Just a stomachache, sir," Ellis gasped.

"Are you sure you haven't been fighting? Don't lie to me."

Ellis shook his head. "Just something I ate."

A heavy frost curled the collard leaves in mid-November. Woodrow's hounds became restless and bayed at night. The evening the moon was half full, Woodrow began lacing the heavy cords of his rubber boots, preparing for the season's first hunt. He worked deliberately, drawing the cords until the rubber crimped. Outside, the hounds yelped and bounded against the wire.

Nadean stood holding a wool muffler. "You better bundle up. It cold as blazes out there."

Woodrow concentrated on lacing his boots.

"Why you want to go out in this cold?" She was bothered that

he was leaving. In their six months together, she had never gone
to bed alone.

"I won't be cold."

Nadean tightened one fist, then released it. "You right sure you
don't want me coming along?" she asked in a timid voice, returning to the question she had asked over supper.

Woodrow shook his head. He tramped to the closet and pulled
out a heavy field jacket. "You ain't got the right clothes," he
finally answered.

Nadean knew there was no use in arguing. Bullheaded old
goat, she thought, feeling mildly rejected. "What time you coming back?"

" 'Fore morning." He pulled the heavy zipper until the coat
closed snug under his chin. Studying Nadean's face, he reached
and traced one finger down her cheek, then tugged her ear. He
picked up his hunting horn, blew a half-year's dust from the
mouthpiece, and hung the rawhide strap over his shoulder. Last,
he lifted his heavy flashlight from the table and walked outside.

Nadean listened to the yelping hounds as they were loaded into
the bed of the truck, then watched the headlights fade into the
night.

"That one strange man," she whispered.

The fire was dying, so Nadean put in another log, stirring the
ashes and banking them against the damp wood. Slowly, flames
licked against the log's beard of lichen and moss. The soft light
cheered her, and she sighed while slumping back in the armchair.

What you care if he go hunting, she thought? He ain't out
getting drunk. Ain't out chasing some woman's ass. Nobody else
have him. You acting plum silly.

Nadean liked how the fire warmed her face. "Let him run
through the woods if he want. Me, I got this nice, warm fire."

Soon, her head bobbed, her thoughts trailed into sleep.

. . . *dreaming*

A small mongrel dop yapped at a cat he had cornered in the

smokehouse—*yap, yap, yap*—one shrill yap followed by another. Nadean listened to the fuss, lying on her back in the wheat field, trying to ignore "uncle's" hand rubbing circles higher and higher on her leg.

"Ain't nothing wrong with it, gal," he urged. "That what it made for."

His teeth gleamed under the bright summer sun. "Uncle" waved the dollar bill. Nadean looked away, back into the clear, high sky. "Mama will whip me if she finds out. She said last time—"

"She ain't gonna find out. Who's gonna tell her? Not me."

"You s'posed to love Mama. You s'posed to do this with the person you love."

"You right. And I love you, same as your mama."

"Uncle's" hand crept to the edge of her panties. He traced one finger along the elastic leg band. "You take this dollar here and buy something pretty." He pressed the bill into her hand.

The dog yapped. A mockingbird scolded the dog from his perch in a gum tree. The dollar was new and crinkled as Nadean's fingers closed. She arched her back as "uncle" slipped her panties down. The crushed, green stalks of wheat tickled her fanny.

Nadean sighed. Why not, anyway? He was always through in just a couple of minutes. Didn't hurt no more, neither. A whole dollar to spend.

"Uncle" lifted his head above the wheat and searched the backyard. Clothes flapping on the line. Smoke coming out the kitchen pipe. Younguns playing dodge ball in the dirt in front of the porch. He crouched on his knees, unzipped his trousers, and took his thing out, shaking it up and down to make it hard.

Teeth grinning like the moon. Glint of saliva on his pink tongue. Nadean looked away from his face into the sky. He drew one of her knees under his arm, jacking her fanny high in the air. Nadean studied a hawk flying high overhead. Two black birds swooped at the hawk.

The dog kept yapping. *Yap, yap.* The cat spit. "Uncle" stuck it in, began wiggling on top of her. The wheat rustled, sounding like someone sweeping the floor. Nadean wished the dog would shut up.

Essie hollered through the back door. "Nadean! Get in here and help with this supper."

Nadean tightened, but "uncle" held her down and wiggled faster. In a few seconds, he was blowing against the side of her neck.

"Nadean," Essie shouted, "where you at girl?" The screen door slammed. Uncle rolled off of her, his thing curling like a crook-neck squash.

"Get out of here," he hissed.

Nadean grabbed her panties from around one ankle, raised her feet in the air trying to slip them on.

"Girl, you better answer me," Essie hollered, coming around the corner of the smokehouse.

"Uncle" pushed her. "Go." She balled her panties in her fist and, crouching, rushed through the wheat toward the woods. The dollar bill slipped from her fingers and disappeared into the tall grain. The dog was yapping and yapping and yapping.

Nadean opened her eyes to find the log engulfed in flames. She was sweating. She rubbed her face, trying to clear the bad dream, confused that she still heard a dog yapping. Oh, it's just Woodrow's hounds she realized.

Nadean sat and listened for several minutes as the sounds of the hunt gained volume in a far wood. She walked to the window and wiped a small circle clear of the dew that had collected on the pane. Across the melon field she could see a few lights still burning in the subdivision.

The sound of the hunt grew urgent, the hounds competing to howl the loudest. Above the cry of the dogs came low, guttural blasts from Woodrow's horn. The duet seemed strange and wild draped over the orderly rest of the community.

Nadean pressed her forehead against the cold pane and wondered if she were forever sentenced to dream of her past. Woodrow's horn sounded again, and she felt a shiver stir in the base of her neck and travel like black snakes down her spine.

"Chase the bad things away from here, Woodrow," she whispered. "Chase them right on out of me."

Benson Bunce was tugged from sleep by the sound of Woodrow's distant horn. He lay still, trying to discover what had awakened him, when again the cold sound of the hunt filtered through his bedroom window.

"Damn it," he whispered. Something about the hunts had disturbed his sleep for years, defying his attempts to plug his ears, sneaking past the pillow over his head and into his mind like a pesky mosquito. Why the sound bothered him, Benson couldn't explain. Sometimes he felt an answer lay barely beneath the membrane covering his brain, drawing and ebbing like a sneeze that won't come.

Why did Woodrow want to hunt alone at night in the first damn place? Hunting was supposed to be a buddy sport, three men walking abreast across a field of cut corn, a covey of quail rising on frantic wings, yanked back to earth with a good eye on a twelve-gauge sight. Hunting was the Saturday morning deer hunts with the club, the barbecue they had at the end of the season. Hunting was not chasing a pack of half-wild dogs through the night, tooting on a horn and waking people up.

Ain't never been a damn thing normal about Woodrow since he was born, Benson thought. Why for God's sake that have to happen to us? He and Porter had hoped that a stint in the army would do Woodrow good, make his mind mature to fit the big body he carried. He was shipped straight off to Vietnam following boot camp, but froze in his first firefight, and was returned in a catatonic state that was broken only after repeated shock therapy.

Margo, Benson's wife, slept curled with her back against him, her breaths as regular as the creak of an oak rocking chair. He had never known her to awaken at the sound of the hunt, and sometimes had the uncomfortable feeling that he was the only person that heard it. Benson tried to divert his attention by thinking about the farm.

Done all right for someone who used to think he wanted to drive trucks. Take off after the war and see the country. Shit, didn't make sense for me to do anything but farm with all this prime land and machinery just waiting. Yeah, I've done all right for a man nearly fifty. Done all right.

Benson kicked, trying to loosen the sheet at his feet. I wish to hell Margo didn't insist on tucking it in so tight, he thought. He pulled the covers down from his bare chest. Woodrow. What the hell me and Porter going to do with him? Living with a damn nigger. Ain't got pride nor sense to fill up a pecan shell. Ought to be committed and socked with that electricity again. Worked pretty good the last time. Why's he acting this way? A man that's going to fool around ought to at least have the common sense to keep it quiet.

Woodrow's horn growled louder as he crested a ridgeline. Margo stirred, pressing her fanny against Benson's leg. Her body was warm and soft as a pillow, but nearly fifteen pounds overweight.

Benson let his mind roll backwards.

Reba's behind had felt firm, the way a sack of grain feels, pushing back when pressed. How long had it been—three years since he last felt that fanny? He had the sense to know when to let something go. But the memory—tight and spongy and hotter than a blowtorch.

Benson had disciplined himself to forget Reba by daylight. Her image in a loose dress with that long, black hair was too distracting for a man in charge of running a farm and family. But in the slow seconds after midnight, her memory was powerful medicine.

They had carried on for more than five years. Nothing ever planned, just getting together when the time was right. She was mixed blood, said she was a Lumbee, had cocoa skin and thick, black hair and a wide mouth that could suck your lips off.

Benson smiled, thinking of the first time he had carried her home from the field after her old man had been sent up for nine years. She said, "Won't you come in, Benson, and have some coffee," and he did, and stayed till midnight.

He rocked his head back and forth on the pillow. It wasn't planned, he told himself. It's a sin when you plan to sin. But God meant a dick for more than just pissing.

She never once asked for money. Sometimes he pressed a few dollars in her hand, bought her a bag of groceries, once some perfume and lacy underwear. She just wanted him, didn't matter if he came by twice a week or once in a month.

Wish she didn't finally turn female on me, Benson lamented. Wanted us to leave and go live together. Farm booming, me with kids and Margo. Man with any sense don't follow his pecker over his brain. Not unless his name is Woodrow.

Benson reached under the covers and patted Margo on her hip. Good damn woman here. I ought to be ashamed of what I'm thinking.

Woodrow's horn sounded again, thin and distant from the far side of the ridge.

That fool Woodrow. The boy just don't understand what he's doing.

□   □   □

Mary woke when the hunt was passing close behind the subdivision. At first she thought she had left the television on. She sat up in bed and listened. After several seconds, she heard the low notes of a horn.

Woodrow's name floated up through the dregs of sleep. Woodrow's hunting. Where had she heard that he hunted alone on some winter nights? One of the dinner parties? She tried to slow her breathing while straining to hear. The horn blew again, strangely harsh, but blending nicely with the pitch of the hounds.

Mary tried to visualize the hunt, but was bothered by the image. Woodrow couldn't possibly be lugging some big gun to shoot a trapped animal from a treetop? From old movies and stories by Faulkner, she knew that type of hunting was popular in the South, but certainly not practiced by one as wise and gentle as Woodrow.

Mary propped against the headboard and listened to the drone of the hunt. The sound was smothered when the dogs threaded patches of woods, gathered volume when ringing across open pastures and fields.

I will hear no gun, Mary told herself. Woodrow is not like most southern men. He is civil and gentle. She concentrated on the baying of the hounds, trying to repel her memory of an earlier hunt.

Mary had hitchhiked for three days across the flat, lonely plains before sighting the edge of the Wyoming Rockies hanging like clouds bunched on the horizon. New England was days and thousands of miles behind her. Her last year of college, the afternoons she had spent in therapy following her emotional breakdown, seemed like a year ago, instead of just two weeks— the Rockies at last, where moose and elk and grizzly bears roamed free. Wild country, a far cry from the dinner parties and luncheons she had endured to please her mother. In those

buckles of earth she planned to find solitude, peace, a new order
where man was the intruder and not in control. The Valiums
she carried in the plastic vial in her pack had nearly turned to
powder. Although she refused to take one, they remained
within reach like a safety net.

Two days of carrying her pack up steep grades, the forest
beside the road too thick to penetrate more than a few yards,
logging trucks rumbling past spewing stinking exhaust. Why
hadn't she taken people's advice and gone to Yellowstone where
there were buses and marked trails? No! She refused to live that
way any longer—be one of the crowd, live to blend in harmoni-
ously with her peers, not make waves or step out of line. She had
done that all of her life while attending prep school, making her
social debut at eighteen, slaving over her books so she would be
admitted to the right college where she would meet and marry a
young man of the right class and breeding. Regardless of the pain
of her breakdown, it had shown her how trivial those values
were, had cleaned out her mind and allowed her for once to stand
up and say no to her parents. And now she would not settle for
tame moose that fed beside the road; she would search until she
found a wild moose.

Two rides. One from an elderly lady who lectured her to live a
life like Jesus, the next from a man who tried to put his hand on
her leg. Just hang in there, girl. Have faith. When Mary Wallace
puts her mind to something, she gets results. I am in search of the
last real moose.

Mary crawled from her tent on the third morning into June air
that still crackled with cold. Her back ached. Feet sore from so
much walking. Wildlife count—two deer, a road-kill raccoon,
and one golden eagle. She longed for a large pizza with everything.

Mary's heart thumped when finally at mid-morning a vehicle
rounded the far curve of the narrow road. She tugged at the straps
on her pack, then stood and lifted one thumb high in the air. The

speck on the road grew into a pickup truck, two figures in the cab, something dark bound to the hood.

The truck passed, both men staring. Mary locked eyes with the driver. Brake lights flared fifty yards past her. Mary's warning bell clanged in her stomach. She didn't trust people who stopped for her only after seeing she was female. She took a heavy breath as the truck's gears scraped into reverse.

"Want a ride?" a young man called from the window when the truck was beside her. He was smiling. Mary nodded briskly. He stepped from the cab and motioned for her to get inside.

In the middle, huh, Mary thought. So you each can feel a leg? She was opening her mouth to say she would ride in the back when she was startled mute by the sight of a large hoof protruding from under the canvas on the hood.

"Hop in," the young man urged. Mary closed her mouth and slid onto the seat, her eyes still riveted on the hoof. The driver nodded his head. Mary felt something hard under one buttock and fished out a shotgun shell.

Both men looked to be in their early twenties, dressed in camouflage jumpsuits with high, leather boots. The driver shifted into first and eased forward, studying Mary from the corner of his eye.

"You ain't afraid to be thumbing alone?" he asked. "I'd beat my sister's behind if I ever caught her thumbing."

Mary's warning bell eased its clamor. The perverts always began by asking if she was cold or if she had a boyfriend. Mary didn't answer, just pointed at the hood.

"What is that?"

"Moose," the driver said. "Young bull." He nodded at the other man. "Tony got him about an hour ago."

"First shot," Tony said, his face opening into a grin. "I sat in that tree stand for two freezing hours, but it paid off."

"You shot a moose!"

"Bet you never seen one, have you?" Tony asked. "Big as a horse. Stop the truck, Joe."

Joe jammed on the brakes. Tony hopped from the cab before the truck had completely stopped. In a moment, he untied a cord and pulled the sheet of canvas aside.

Except for an occasional dead animal on the highway, Mary had never seen death. All four grandparents were still living, the beef and chicken she grew up eating was always cooked and carved before meeting her plate. She sucked in her breath at the sight of the dead animal.

His eyes were open and shone with the flat gleam of still water. Behind the front leg was a neat, slightly oval tear, the edges of skin turned in. The exposed flesh was purple. The hair surrounding the wound was shiny with thick, drying blood. Several flies rested on the animal's nose. The moose looked as if it were made of plastic, as lifeless as a picture in a book.

"Why did you kill him?" Mary asked softly.

"Why? Because I was hunting." Tony hunched one shoulder. "That's what you do with moose, you hunt them."

Her memory of what happened next was fuzzy—a sob spilled from her lips, her crying becoming uncontrollable until she was screaming at the two men, slapping at them, clawing and biting. Blackness followed, her next recollection the hospital room where the cloud lifted, her mother bent holding her hand.

Mary's mind drew back to the present with another long bellow from Woodrow's horn. The dead moose returned to the tight capsule where she kept all thoughts of wildness and rebellion.

Mary shuddered and rested her hand on Jeffery's back. He always slept so soundly.

I believe in Woodrow. There will be no gunshot. She drifted into restless sleep.

□ □ □

Mack Lupo sucked on a Marlboro, blowing the smoke through his open truck window. The cool air felt good on his face. Wedged between his knees was a tall Budweiser. Parked on the shoulder of the road, a half mile from the edge of Oak Hills, he listened to the sounds of night—an owl hooting from a nearby treetop, a lone rooster crowing, probably scared from his roost by a possum, the baying of Woodrow's hounds.

Mack was on his third beer and the alcohol was beginning to kick in, his pulse was slowing. The tension of the drive was melting. Pulled it off again, he thought, a smile turning up the corners of his mouth. Again he touched his trouser pocket and felt the thick roll of hundred-dollar bills. He knew he would sleep well tonight, then tomorrow even-up with his two brothers. His split would be enough to catch the bills up and still have a nest egg to ease Nancy and the kids through winter. Straight farming just didn't cut it any longer.

The Lupo brothers had farmed all their lives, but never enjoyed the success of the Bunces'. If drought didn't get them, it was a hailstorm. And when one crop did come off good, the market price would fall to rock bottom. But Mack brought a scheme back from Nam, and for the past nine years he and his brothers had grown a little dope on the ridges above Oak Hills. Nothing big time, just a hundred or so plants scattered through the forest, tended well and harvested at peak sap. They hung the plants up to cure in an old tobacco barn. The crop was sold in bulk to a fellow in Raleigh, nobody got hurt, and the bills got paid.

Mack opened another can of beer. The sound of baying hounds had drowned out the owl. Run on, crazy man, he thought. You do your thing, I'll do mine. There's room on that ridge for the two of us.

□   □   □

Ellis's left testicle and all of his ribs were still aching from the fight as he lay in bed staring at the dark ceiling.

I'll get that son of a bitch, he thought. Somehow, someday. Carefully, he felt his testicle, some swelling, a bruise, but nothing busted.

When the baying of the hounds reached his window, Ellis was not startled. He had lived in Oak Hills long enough to expect the hunts soon after the weather turned cold.

Strange fucker, Ellis thought. I can't figure him out. He don't never kill an animal. Won't let me come with him. What's he do, run through the woods holding his dick? Ain't no telling, knowing Woodrow.

Despite his queerness, Ellis had grown to like the big man. Although Woodrow towered above him by more than a foot, he spoke to Ellis in a manner that made him feel they looked at each other eye to eye.

"Why are you so short?" Woodrow asked him once.

"What happened to your folks?" Woodrow asked another time.

Both questions had brought color to Ellis's face, but he appreciated the interest. Most adults either ignored him or treated him as a child. Woodrow spoke his mind.

Ellis also thought of Woodrow as an orphan. He had a family, but had spent most of his life alone. Once while hoeing the melons, Ellis had asked Woodrow how it had been growing up with wealthy parents. Woodrow stopped chopping at a tuft of nut grass, his poker face wrinkling with thought.

"I had a tree fort in a chinaberry tree behind the house. Built it myself. Dad cut the tree down so he could build a new barn."

Ellis shared Woodrow's memory of loss in recalling his childhood. He could not even remember his mother's face, only scraps of events when he was very small. One incident stuck in his mind.

They were walking down a road, Ellis, his mother, and two other children. His mother held a crying infant. She handed Ellis a glass bottle half filled with milk. The nipple smelled sour. Ellis watched his mother lift the baby against her shoulder and pat him, whispering, "Hush baby, hush baby." Ellis stared at the bottle, then let it slip between his fingers. The bottle turned sideways as it fell, shattering against the pavement. He remembered the puddle of milk soaking into the dust, the bright shards of glass, his mother shouting at him, her face black against the sun.

Ellis listened as the hunt grew loud close to the Home, then slowly faded in volume as the hounds passed over a ridge. Woodrow may be a crazy bastard, Ellis thought, but he does his own thing. Doesn't give a hoot what other people think.

Carefully, Ellis rolled from his bed, pressing a fist against his groin. You'll get yours, Billy. He felt for the windowsill, steadied himself, then slid the window open a few inches. Cold air spilled in. Ellis cupped his hands to shield the flare of a match, then lit a cigarette. He blew the smoke outside. 'Bout time I start doing my own thing, Ellis thought. I'm heading out west.

Ellis counted the time until his birthday. In seventy-three days, he would turn eighteen, reach adulthood, and become a free man.

The hunt crested another ridge. Ellis heard one last growl from Woodrow's horn before returning to his bed and sleep. He dreamed of far mountains, the twitter of morning birds in a desert bush.

utumn passed into winter. A freak snowstorm covered Oak Hills in early December. The Christmas buying season saw the sale of five new homes in the subdivision in just one week.

Woodrow and Nadean's relationship was now either accepted or ignored by the townspeople of Oak Hills. The older Bunce brothers decided to wait Woodrow out until they had sufficient reason to have him committed. Most of the local merchants actually encouraged the odd couple to stop by, liking Woodrow's quickness to buy anything Nadean showed an interest in.

Woodrow and Nadean remained as symbols of liberalism to the residents of the subdivision, but the fervor of having them visit passed, just as the crazes died for backgammon and Trivial Pursuit. Most days, Woodrow and Nadean stayed on the tiny farm and were glad for the privacy, tired of discussing nuclear war, politics, and the fate of the eagles.

The winter garden flourished under Nadean's careful eye. Ellis came once a week to help with whatever chores Woodrow came up with. Nadean chuckled at the sight of the two working, a giant and midget, Ellis sneaking peeks at her when he thought she wouldn't notice.

Nadean continued to flourish in the clean life without mirrors. Slowly returned the figure she had carried before the years on dope, her hair grew thick and shiny, the color of her skin matched a clean penny. She gave up wearing bright reds and yellows for rich greens and browns, the colors of the earth. Her skirts were long and loose, allowing the wind to swirl around her ankles. She went shoeless when the sun warmed the ground, the scars on her arms slowly fading against her skin. Standing gazing across the field at the end of the day, her face tilted, a breeze tugging her curls and the hem of her skirt, she seemed to be scooped from the earth and molded from the clay and rich soil of Oak Hills.

Sometimes while working, Nadean caught herself singing one of the sad love ballads she remembered from Washington. She would stop, as if afraid any ties with that bad time would draw her back.

No, you being silly, girl, she reassured herself. These new times. Old times are gone. You just be like old Woodrow and don't care. People done took all they can take.

□   □   □

OCTOBER 1969

Nadean stepped with wide eyes from the bus in Washington, toting a worn cardboard-and-cloth suitcase and fifty-seven dollars she had slipped from the current "uncle's" trouser pocket. She wore a floral-print cotton dress, her hair tied in a red scarf, just one week past her sixteenth birthday.

"Lord, what I do now," she whispered, turning slowly to follow the stream of strange faces rushing past. She felt her breast pocket, where a scrap of paper held the address of her aunt. She had no telephone number and had not taken time to write first. The address she carried was copied from a year-old letter.

Nadean's eyes ached when she emerged from the depot onto the bright street. She shaded her eyes with her palm, saw a street that was wider than a river, buildings taller than any she had seen even in Raleigh.

"Lord, girl, you ain't even close to home," she whispered.

The noises were frightening. Nadean could only distinguish sounds for a second, the honk of a car swallowed by the swoosh of a passing bus, the thud of empty oil drums being loaded on a truck silenced under the chatter of a jackhammer, a man shouting "Pretzels. Hot pretzels," his mouth suddenly moving in silence as a jet rose overhead. The noises combined into a steady drone that peaked and ebbed and peaked.

No one smiled. People rushed past Nadean with their eyes scouting the concrete. The few who even glanced at her averted their eyes when she smiled. Back home, even white people would speak.

Nadean wandered for more than an hour, trying to match the letters on street signs to the name on her scrap of paper. Finally, she gathered the courage to ask directions from a policeman standing on a corner. He paused, staring at the sprigs of her hair leaking from the scarf, then turned and pointed, gesturing as he talked. Another jet was rising over the building tops, and the only word that Nadean caught was "subway."

Subway? Nadean had heard of subways, but finding one and riding it was another story. She thanked the policeman and hurried away. She was hungry, not having eaten since the night before when she gobbled two pieces of cold fried chicken before slipping out the back door. She smelled food, turned and saw another man shouting "Pretzels" from beside his small wagon.

What's a pretzel? she thought. Don't matter, he say they hot.

Nadean handed the man a dollar, and he handed her something that resembled a doughnut. Nadean waited a moment for change, but got none, then nibbled at one edge. What in the world? Tasted like hard bread and salt. She dropped it in a trash barrel.

She first spied Jerome leaning against a lamp post at the corner of two of the wide streets. He was tall and lanky, wearing a powder blue suit with wide lapels, and a wide-brimmed hat. His wide mustache was trimmed like a knife edge along the top of his lip. He was the most beautiful man that she had ever seen. Suddenly, she realized that he was staring back at her, smiling, happy lines running from the corners of his eyes. Nadean jerked her eyes from him.

"Hey, babe," the man called. "You look like you just lost your puppy." He spoke southern, not exactly like she and the folks from Oak Hills talked, but different from the clipped speech of people here. Nadean looked up from the sidewalk and found him still smiling.

Maybe he can tell me how to get to Auntie's house? Nadean wondered. She pulled the paper from her pocket and walked toward him. "I . . . I'm sorry to bother you, sir, but I'm new here and I—"

"New around here? Naw," he kidded. "You look like you were born in D.C."

Nadean blushed and held up the scrap of paper. "You know where this street is? I got folks there."

The man looked Nadean over from head to feet, the tip of his tongue playing with the corner of his mustache. Nadean noticed the large diamond he wore on his pinkie. Maybe he a movie star? she wondered.

"Yeah, yeah," he nodded. "I know this street. Way 'cross town."

"Sir, you reckon you could tell me how to get there? Policeman say something 'bout a subway."

The man chuckled. "Babe, I bet you never seen a subway in your whole life, have you?"

Nadean lowered her face. She was ashamed of her loose, homemade dress, scuffed sandals, the fact that she had never seen a subway. She shook her head. "No."

Nadean was surprised when the man lifted her chin with his hand. "Hey, I was just funning with you. What's your name?"

"Nadean. Nadean Tucker."

He tipped his hat. "Jerome here. Jerome Blue."

"I'm pleased to meet you."

Jerome rolled the scrap of paper into a tight ball between his fingers. "Where you from, honey?"

"North Carolina. Little place called Oak Hills."

"Yeah? I'm from South Carolina. Been a while, though. Listen here, home girl, you way too pretty to be stumbling around trying to find the subway. People 'round here ain't so nice like they be in the South."

Jerome flicked the ball of paper into the gutter. "I know the part of town where your people live. How 'bout me giving you a ride as a welcoming present?"

Jerome pointed at a long, late-model Lincoln Continental parked up the block. Nadean sucked in her breath at the thought of riding in such a car. "I don't want to be such a bother."

Jerome reached and rested his hand on her shoulder. "Ain't no bother. Come on," his smile bright like the sun. "Welcome to the big city."

The big car rode so smoothly, Nadean felt as if she were floating. She rubbed her fingers across the white leather interior. The polished hood reflected lamp posts and stoplights.

Wish them hicks back home could see me now, Nadean thought. Their tongues be hanging below their chin.

Jerome drove fast down the wide avenue, cut into a side street, into another, over a bridge, ducked yellow lights, until soon Nadean had no sense of east or west. He drove sitting low in his seat, one big hand guiding the car, telling her of his arrival in Washington ten years ago after leaving the farm.

"Got to hustle in the city. Got to," he said. "Else people will walk right over you. Ain't nobody gonna give you shit."

Nadean studied her reflection in the chromed glove compartment door. She felt ashamed at her wispy hair, the fake gold chain around her neck. "What kind'a work you do?" she asked.

"Making a buck. That's my business. Entertainment, mostly."

Nadean felt her heart jump. Maybe he famous?

Jerome slowed the car as he turned into a littered street lined with gray buildings. People sat on doorsteps, looked up with indifference, then back to their game of cards, checkers, or bottle of wine. Trash cans were turned over, dogs eating the garbage. Two cats spit at each other from sides of an alley.

This place ugly, Nadean thought. This what they call the ghetto? What we doing here?

Jerome slowed in front of a building, then stopped. He leaned to peer through the window, shook his head, and whistled softly.

"Huh, huh, huh, honey, looks bad. Looks real bad."

"What you mean?"

Jerome pointed at the door to the building. It was nailed closed with wide boards. A condemned sign was tacked to the wood.

"I mean it looks like your folks ain't here no more. City's done closed the building."

Nadean felt fear curdle in her stomach, and for a moment she feared she would be sick. She choked back a sob. "But I got to find her. She the only person I know here. You sure this is the right place?" With her ignorance of Washington, she did not realize he had driven her to the wrong quadrant.

Jerome nodded. He pointed at the number on the building. "Look at the address yourself. People come and go in D.C. Especially in this part of town."

Nadean could not stop her sob this time, and it spilled from her mouth, causing her shoulders to jerk. She covered her face with her hands. "Oh what in the world I gonna do," she moaned. "What am I gonna do?"

Nadean felt Jerome's hand on the back of her neck. "Hey, now, stop that crying. You know me, don't ya? What you say I put you up at my crib a couple'a nights? Long enough for you to locate your aunt."

That first day in Washington now seemed to Nadean like it was dredged from some past century. On her knees between two rows of collards, she ceased to care about white leather seats, long city nights, and smoky jazz clubs.

Damn the past, she told herself. Ain't no sense in dwelling on what you were, who you weren't. Don't worry 'bout the future neither, just cut these collards and worry 'bout buying a ham hock to cook them with.

Enzor stared across his desk at Ellis, who squirmed on the edge of his chair.

"Okay, let me get this straight," he said. "You're going to

leave, just like that. Quit school with three months left before
you graduate and take off for God knows where."

Ellis nodded. He coughed into his fist. "I've thought about it
long and hard, sir, and I've—I've made up my mind."

Enzor bounced his pencil on its eraser. "Well, I will say you
have made one hell of a decision. One HELL-OF-A-DECI-
SION. Going to just take off, not a penny to your name, quit
school, all these decisions made with the great maturity that
comes one day after turning eighteen. I would call that one hell of
a decision, McDonald!"

Ellis jiggled his foot, coughed again. "Well, sir, that is my
decision. I'm legal age now. I don't give a flip about hanging
around here another day."

Enzor dropped his pencil and leaned forward over his desk.
"Son, I just can't believe that after living here for fourteen years,
you can just walk away without one thought for your future.
Didn't I teach you any better than that?"

"I'm grateful for everything you've done for me, Mr. Enzor.
But, I want to go."

Enzor sighed, then pushed his chair back from the desk. "Well,
you are eighteen, son. I wish to God you weren't. But, I can't stop
you from leaving." Enzor rose in his chair and walked to the
window. He was silent for several seconds, then turned around. "I
think today, Ellis, you are making the first major mistake of your
life."

Ellis slowly packed his suitcase. A knot of boys watched from
the end of his bunk. There wasn't much to pack—an outfielder's
glove, four changes of clothes, a broken Garcia spin reel. His bank
sock was fat with nearly five hundred dollars.

None of the other boys spoke; they were all stunned into
silence. Never could anyone remember one of the fellows just
packing up and leaving as soon as he turned eighteen. Even
Billy Williams with his bragging and hot temper had never up
and left.

Ellis snapped closed the latch on his suitcase, then lifted it to test the weight. He leaned over his bunk and smoothed a wrinkle in the spread, staring at the cube of space he had called home, then wheeled around.

"See you suckers in Hollywood," Ellis said, grasping the handle of his bag. He raised to his full stature and began marching toward the door.

"Bye, Ellis," a strained, lone voice called. "Yeah, see you, man," another said.

Ellis said goodbye to no one, did not even look back until he was out the door and a quarter mile down the road.

A chill wind was blowing from the west. Ellis sucked gobs of the air, trying to swallow the knot that ached in his throat. He set his mind on watching clouds scurry across the sky. He hoped to at least make Raleigh before nightfall. There, he figured he would get a cheap motel room—hell no, an expensive one—and decide where he was heading. He fastened the top button on his coat and bent into the wind.

I'll just follow this breeze and see where it comes from. Ellis imagined the wind's source as high on the crest of a snow-capped mountain, gushing from the bowels of an ice-blue glacier. He pictured the wind dancing in a cold swirl upon the ice, before sliding over the edge of the mountain and barreling down the side, rolling across the plains where it swelled into the cold hand that slapped his face. Ellis focused on the image of high, beautiful mountains and fought a strong urge to turn around.

Ellis had one detour on his odyssey westward. He wanted to say goodbye to Woodrow.

Big dumb fucker probably don't give a shit now that he's got that live-in coon. Still, I reckon I ought to tell him I can't work for him any longer.

Ellis climbed the hill to Woodrow's house. He blew his nose, combed his hair with his fingers, then knocked on the door. Nadean opened the door and stared at his suitcase.

"Hello, Ellis. You going on vacation?"

Ellis dropped the suitcase on the porch. Inside, he nodded at Woodrow, then marched to the stove and poured himself a cup of coffee.

"Yeah, I reckon you could call it vacation. Permanent vacation."

Nadean lifted one eyebrow at Woodrow. Woodrow rose from his seat and walked to stand by the young man's side. Nadean brought Ellis's bag inside. It reminded her of the battered suitcase she had toted out of Oak Hills.

"Ain't no school today?" Woodrow asked.

"Not for me. I turned eighteen yesterday. I'm heading for the West."

Ellis took a cigarette from a pack in his front pocket and lit it. The flare of sulfur smoke made his eyes water. He squinted, drawing his lungs full. "I just wanted to stop by and say bye to ya'll."

Woodrow took a toothpick from an empty tabasco sauce bottle. He stuck the tip between two bottom teeth. "Say that again." The toothpick bobbed. "You're quitting school and going west?"

Ellis did not think Woodrow's range of vocabulary included arguments or lectures, but by the way his eyes locked onto Ellis's own, he knew the big man had been stirred.

"I've thought about it, Woodrow. For months now. I been in that home since I was a baby and have hated every minute. I'm a man now, and it's time to move on."

"Where you plan on going?"

"I ain't sure yet. Maybe California."

"How you plan on getting there? What you going to eat?"

"I'll do all right. I've got some money. I can work, too. Maybe pick oranges or something. Main thing is, I'll be on my own."

"This can't wait till school is out?"

Ellis sucked hard at his cigarette, filling his lungs till they stung. He exhaled a stream of irritation with the smoke.

"Jesus Christ, Woodrow. I thought if anybody would understand, you would." Ellis crushed the butt in the sink, then lifted his hand. "I just wanted to stop and say bye."

Nadean's stare followed Ellis's leg to his pants cuff where an inch of skin showed. Finally starting to grow, she thought. Now he'll sprout up like a weed. Looks so cocky standing there, all ready to jump on the whole world. Makes me want to slap him hard, make him open his eyes. Lord, honey, if you only knew. I could tell you some things about the world.

Woodrow grasped Ellis's hand for several seconds. "Reckon you're old enough to make up your own mind. Eighteen, huh?" Woodrow released his hand. "Let's walk out to the field."

Ellis opened his mouth to say no, but stopped when he saw how serious and clear Woodrow's eyes were. "I need to be going soon."

The wind was still cold, but the sun had inched higher and the air was warming. A couple of early robins sunned on the withered grass.

"You're a man now," Woodrow said. "That's plain enough. Watched you grow up right in front of me."

Woodrow walked to the middle of his front lawn and stood gazing down on the skeletons of two houses under construction. "You consider hiring on with me for a couple of months?" he asked Ellis.

"I can't."

"I'm going to need a full-time man for a while," Woodrow continued as if he had not heard Ellis. "Got plans. Nadean wants a palm tree. Might haul some sand in here and build a beach."

Ellis could not stop the corners of his mouth from lifting. "That's the craziest damn thing I ever heard, Woodrow. You can't grow palm trees in North Carolina." Ellis also knew that Woodrow never kidded.

Woodrow continued his monotone. "I'll pay you good wages, give you a room and food."

Ellis conjured up an image of the beach, then chuckled. Palm trees and white sand here in the hill country of middle Carolina. All those new people with their fancy houses would shit.

"How long you expecting this project will take?"

"Two, three months at the most. Want it in time for warm weather."

Push on, a little voice urged Ellis. Get the hell on out of this hick town.

A louder voice. Spring isn't here yet. That glacier on the mountain has been there thousands of years. Two more months won't matter. The wind can still guide you.

Ellis thrust out his hand. "Woodrow, I wouldn't miss this for the world."

Following supper that night, Ellis sat alone in his new bedroom absorbing the strange feeling of having so much space. He opened his suitcase and placed a piece of clothing in each dresser drawer so it would seem full. He lay his baseball glove on a shelf, his rod and reel in the center of a card table, set his shoes beside the door. Ellis rolled across the double mattress, amazed at how many turns it took to reach from side to side. No curfew, no bed checks. No fights or farting contests. No asshole calling him pygmy. He lay on the floor in the middle of the room for several minutes just for the hell of it. No one would say no.

Through the door, he heard muffled conversation between Nadean and Woodrow. Bet she's giving him hell, he mused. Probably wants me to leave already. Well, lady, I won't be here long. Couple of months at most. Don't matter if I'm not heading west right yet. I'm on my own. Making my own decisions.

Later Ellis heard a tap on the door and involuntarily stiffened and shouted, "Yes, sir." He felt silly when Nadean poked her head through the door.

"We fixing to go to bed. You need some extra covers or something more to eat?"

"No, ma'am," Ellis answered.

"You mind if I come into your room for a minute?"

Ellis bent and smoothed a wrinkle from the bedspread. "No, ma'am."

Nadean seated herself in a wooden chair. "You stop that 'ma'am' stuff. Call me Nadean."

Ellis nodded. Nadean worked her fingers together as she clasped her hands in her lap.

"You smart, Ellis," she said. "A sight smarter than I was at your age. I was like one of them little calves that run in a circle fast as it can."

"What you mean?"

Nadean picked at a sliver of dead skin at the edge of one nail. "I mean you take time to think. You gonna stay on and finish school. Make something of your life. Me, I can't even read nothing 'cept my name."

Ellis looked away from Nadean's black eyes into the pattern of the bedspread. He had wondered since his decision to stay if he would be expected to return to school, and now he felt a sense of near relief.

"You made me think of myself when you came in toting that suitcase. I left Oak Hills just like that, bound and certain to get my piece of the pie."

"You've done all right," Ellis said, looking back into her face. "At least you've been places. I've never been out of this state."

"Oh, I've done. I ain't going to say I've done all right, but I've done. Ashamed of most of it. Still can't read."

"Reading ain't everything."

"Not till you can't do it. Then it gets more important. You learn to read real good, Ellis. Learn all them fancy words. Maybe some day 'fore you leave here, you can teach me some."

Nadean wrung her hands. "Well, I better be getting in bed. Woodrow be cold all alone."

Nadean stood over Ellis for a moment, then quickly stooped and kissed his cheek. "We a family, Ellis. Lord knows, a mixed-up lot, but we a family."

In the dark afterward, Ellis stifled his sobs against the soft belly of a pillow.

With moderate embarrassment, Ellis returned to school and faced the fellows after his bold exit for the West. He was surprised to find that even Billy Williams greeted him, and listened with the others of his diversion by Woodrow. Most boys felt that living inside Woodrow's pagan life-style was even more alluring than cresting the Continental Divide.

"No shit, a room all to yourself. Really?"

"And you can turn in whenever you want to? Don't have to do your homework unless you feel like it?"

"That black woman. She really sleeping with Mr. Bunce?"

Ellis enjoyed his growth of popularity nearly as much as he enjoyed his increasing height. In only three weeks after leaving the Home, he found his trouser cuffs getting short. His legs often ached, and his voice had taken to sliding the range of a kazoo. Inside, he felt a strange, tingling energy like low fever; he thought often of the melon vines pushing toward sunlight from the rich soil.

Ellis also discovered that his earlier jealousy of Nadean was unwarranted. She was Woodrow's bedmate, but he and the big man continued their strange friendship. Woodrow seemed to radiate a measured aura of personality and attention that spread an even three hundred and sixty degrees. Woodrow would be Woodrow would be Woodrow. Ellis even began to like the quiet woman. She had called him family.

11

"It's a sight," said Miss Penny from the door of her restaurant, her mouth agape as the palm rolled down Main Street on the bed of a tractor trailer. "Come here and look at this, Eunice," she called over her shoulder to a woman waiting tables.

The thirty-foot palm lay with a slight curve down the length of the trailer, the root ball bound in burlap, the fronds taped together to keep them from flapping. As the truck passed the shops and houses, doors swung open and people flocked outside to watch. Several young boys trailed behind on bicycles.

Woodrow and Ellis were expecting the tree. Woodrow had

ordered it three weeks earlier after Ellis found an advertisement in a magazine. The astonished plant nursery owner in Florida finally agreed to dig up and ship the tree after Woodrow wired him five hundred dollars in cash.

The day was Saturday, Woodrow, Nadean, and Ellis chomping at a large breakfast when they heard the commotion coming up the street. Nadean cocked her head and listened to the low growl of gears, the excited chatter of children that now almost surrounded the truck. "What in the world that be?" she asked, standing and walking to the front window. "Lord God!" she exclaimed. "Woodrow, come and look."

Ellis was up in a flash, ripping the curtain aside. "It's the palm, Woodrow!" he exclaimed. "Look at that thing."

Woodrow wiped his mouth on a napkin and rose slowly, giving his half-finished plate a sad look. Ellis bolted through the door, leaving it open behind him. Through the gap, Woodrow watched the truck grind to a stop under the direction of pointing children. Several cars also pulled to the side of the road. "Damn, it's long," Woodrow said, a smile slowly lighting his face.

"That thing coming here?" Nadean asked, moving close to Woodrow and taking his hand. "What in the world is going on?"

"You said you wanted a beach," Woodrow answered. "One with palm trees." He looked into her eyes and nodded toward the truck.

"What—you can't—Woodrow," Nadean squealed, her hands flapping like birds. She started off the front porch, then ran back to Woodrow, jumped and hugged him around his neck, then rushed back toward the steps. "You are *craaazy,* Woodrow," she shouted over her shoulder.

In less than fifteen minutes, probably a quarter of the population of Oak Hills was assembled on Woodrow's front lawn. Woodrow paced around his house several times, followed by a throng of the curious, studying the slope and measure of his land.

Finally, he pushed a stick into the dirt at a gentle knob in the center of his front yard.

"Best drainage here," he explained to Ellis. Ellis looked down the hill toward the many houses of the subdivision.

Woodrow directed the truck up his lawn to the selected site of the beach. The driver looked with amazement at the milling, jabbering crowd, then climbed from his cab and began loosening the nylon straps that bound the tree.

Twenty men and boys lifted the palm gently from the trailer and laid it prone on the grass. Nadean fussed like a mother hen, shooing children back from the fronds while she soaked the root ball with water from a hose. More of the curious arrived. Woodrow and Ellis broke into the cold earth with a mattock and shovel, and were joined by other townsmen, some digging with only their hands. Noon had just chimed on the church bell when Woodrow stopped digging and announced that the hole was large enough. He took his wallet from his trousers and handed one of the boys three twenties, then instructed him to fetch all the ham bisquits and sodas that Miss Penny had in stock.

Ropes were tied high on the trunk of the palm, the tree walked skyward like raising a flag. The root ball slid with a solid thump into the hole. Woodrow and two of the heavier men steadied her, while others scurried to pack dirt around the base of the palm and plug her to the rich earth of Oak Hills.

At last, a hush fell over the crowd as they stared with awe at palm fronds rustling against the blue sky. Nadean, squinting her eyes, could easily imagine she stood in white sand before ocean breakers. Miss Penny broke the silence when she arrived in her ancient Chrysler, the back seat filled with steaming sacks of ham biscuits and several crates of cold Pepsi. A picnic ensued, folks sitting on the grass and eating, between mouthfuls still wondering why Woodrow wanted a palm tree on his front lawn.

"I can die now," one of the old farmers said. "I've seen it all. There's a palm tree in Oak Hills."

"Well, it ain't no magnolia," another answered. "Kind'a reminds me of a tobacco plant."

Against the soft contours of the surrounding oaks, the palm looked reptilian, as startling as if a dinosaur had crawled from the hole, as bold against the horizon as a forearm and fist held aloft.

The sun inched into the western sky. A dove swooped in, but suddenly veered from the strange shape.

"You think you'd ever see a palm tree in Oak Hills?" one of the old-timers asked another.

"No," he answered, looking down the hill toward the new houses of the subdivision. "I didn't. But it doesn't surprise me much. Nothing around here surprises me now."

The mild day ended with a cold wind that blew out of the northwest. After hearing a weather forecast, Nadean paced the living room floor.

"All the damn nights to call for a record low," she fussed. "You'd think that kind'a mess be over."

"Build a fire," Ellis said. "That's what the orange growers do in Florida."

"We have to do something," she said. "Weak as she is, ain't no way she live otherwise."

Woodrow heaved to his feet and plodded outside to begin splitting firewood. Ellis reached for his coat, but Nadean stopped him.

"You go on and get your homework done. Get to bed. There only three months between you and a diploma. This here's my silliness. I'll tend to it."

Ellis protested, but Nadean shooed him toward his room. She dressed in several layers of shirts and trousers, then added a coat and ski cap. From outside, she heard the cadence of Woodrow's ax.

They piled split oak at four corners around the palm. Woodrow soaked the wood with kerosene, then lit the fires. The flames licked up, throwing twisted shadows against the front of the house.

Woodrow and Nadean stood together in the circle of light, hand in hand. In the harsh glow, the trunk of the palm looked even taller and skinnier, curving into the darkness like the blade of a knife. The hounds bayed.

After midnight had passed, Nadean fussed Woodrow into the house. "No, I ain't hearing of it," she said. "Two of us out here be double the fool." She jabbed her finger at his chest, backing him toward the porch. " 'Sides, you get sick, I'd have to call a horse doctor to come."

Nadean sat on an upturned bucket, huddled under the folds of a quilt. Occasionally, she shone a flashlight beam into the palm. If the fronds were not stirred by currents of warm air, she added more wood to the fire.

People looking at this palm like it a ghost or something, Nadean mused. Ain't nothing but another tree. Why it have to look the same as all the rest? I don't look like Woodrow. Them new Jap people down the road don't look like me. Like they say, live and let live.

She stood and stretched, then walked to the palm and laid her hands on the trunk. Warm. She slipped one hand under her coat and felt her belly. Warm.

"You my baby," she whispered. "Me and Woodrow's baby. We gonna look after you, feed you and watch you grow. We'll figure out the problems as they come."

Nadean returned to her seat and warmed her hands before the flames. "The money girl long gone," she said to the night. "Dead and gone." The dance of the flames drew her mind back to an earlier time.

□   □   □

Nadean heard the low notes of the saxophone in the Zodiac Club back in Washington.

"Just sing like you sing to me," Jerome told her behind the curtain. "Pretend we just walking in the park."

Blue smoke hung over the room. Nadean smelled spilled beer, cigarettes, and warm hair dressing. She hoped she wouldn't get sick. She clung to the microphone stand, fearing her knees would buckle if she released her grip. Her tongue felt thick as a biscuit.

Jerome took his seat at the front table, cocked his head to one side, and smiled at her, his gold tooth looking big as the moon. Sing, he mouthed at her, after the sax had twice passed her cue.

Nadean pushed out one word. That word towed another. After only a few bars, the biscuit melted, and it was like she was singing in the church choir, she was home, walking the banks of the Haw River, a young girl. The cigarette smoke was really morning fog, the beer bottles were flowers beaded with dew. She sang about falling in love with the boy who lived across the field, his lips sweet like candy, narrowed her eyes till all the faces were flowers, sang to those flowers the old songs she remembered.

Heard clapping like thunder. Flowers can't clap. Nadean opened her eyes and saw people smiling at her, beating their hands together. Backstage, the man handed her a crisp fifty and told her to come back the next week.

The few good years. Nadean became a regular in the jazz joints around D.C. Jerome knew all the club owners, saw to it she was paid right, dressed her in uptown clothes, had fliers printed with her picture and name. The tobacco fields and toilets of home were just part of some bad dream.

Jerome kept her well, big ole apartment, carpet, waterbed with colored lights, a Doberman they walked in the park. Jerome with that big roll of bills in his pocket, cruising the city half the night, women who called—can't get too nosey, man has to hustle in the city. He had explained that. You my main squeeze, but a man has got to hustle. Nobody give you nothing. He kept her well.

Kept plenty of dope, too.

"Marijuana? Shit. Ain't nothing to it," he said. "Make you feel good. That's all."

She was afraid. One of the "uncles" had a brother who got hooked on dope and turned up dead in an alley in New York. Dope kill you.

Jerome lit the joint. The paper flamed, then settled to a red ash. The odor reminded her of burning rubber. He sucked in three short breaths, held them, then slowly exhaled.

"Try it, baby."

Nadean shook her head.

"Come on now. You think Jerome give you something bad?"

Nadean stared at the joint like looking at a snake. Dope kill you, the "uncle" had whispered. No, Jerome wouldn't hurt me, she reasoned. Not this man. Nadean gagged on the first puff.

"No. Go easy, like this." Jerome sucked on the joint like sucking a straw.

"You right. This stuff like candy," Nadean said a couple of minutes later when the joint was finished. An intoxication was settling over her, but different from beer or scotch. She was floating, colors bright, the stereo booming like it was a real band.

"Dope just makes the good times better," Jerome said.

For Nadean, dope did make the good times better. It also helped ease the bad times.

Home was a long way from the streets of Washington. Nadean woke to the drone of traffic instead of songbirds. When the rain fell, the city was as gray as a coffin, the cold tunneling like tiny bugs under her clothes. Maybe Mama had beat her, but she had hugged her even more, and no one could hug like Mama. Not even Jerome. For all her hated memories of tobacco gum on her hands, of squatting to pee in the edge of the weeds, she still couldn't shake her recall of snatching a tiny, flapping perch from the fishing pond, of sucking the stems of sweet honeysuckle blossoms, of crawling into the bed with Mama when the thunder boomed too close. Often Nadean wished she could write a letter home or had the courage to phone.

But she could sing. With a few tokes of reefer, a little hash, she could sing away the rain, turn the tired faces into pools of quiet water. She transformed herself into an old girlfriend, Mama's warm hug, that boy who vowed to return from the service, a good afternoon spent fishing on a lake, the flight of a red balloon above treetops against the sky.

Suck that hash pipe, the audience whispered. Sing on, songbird. Carry us all home.

. . . Jerome caught in bed with one of his whores.

"Aw baby, she don't mean shit to me," he pleaded. "She pales to pure shit side'a you."

Cutting two thick lines of coke on a mirror. "Here, try this. Make you forget about her. Some of my best shit."

Nadean examined herself as she leaned over the mirror. Red puffy eyes. Hair needs ironing. Ugly damn hick. She squinted her eyes and snorted a line deep into each nostril. Felt like a rocket taking off. Made her lips turn up, smile like some happy old cow.

You still pretty, girl, she thought, lowering her head for another line. Prettier than any damn whore.

. . . Jerome slapping her for talking with another man. Cussing her. Nadean tasted blood. Felt the jagged edge of a tooth. One eye closed, a knot over her cheek swelled big as a plum. Jerome standing over her holding a needle, tears shiny on his face.

"Baby, I didn't mean it. You can't leave me. I just get so mad sometimes. Like I can't control myself."

He knelt beside her, rubbing her shoulder. Nadean stared at the light dancing on the tip of the needle.

"You just relax, honey, and let me make it up to you," Jerome whispered. "Jerome make you feel good."

Not many months passed before Nadean needed a needle to go onstage. One to put her to sleep at night. The world was just too

sad, all those faces staring at her. Everybody expecting the songbird to lead them home.

. . . Nadean rocking back and forth on a mattress, her belly
cramped hard as rock. Jerome with his shiny needle standing over
her. Not smiling now.

"Bitch won't sing no more got to find another way to earn her
keep."

Nadean tried to swallow, choked, then nodded. "Hear me? I
ain't joking. Ain't no free rides in the city. Everybody got to earn
their keep."

But singing became impossible in a world where all the birds
had flown south, a city where bright spring flowers, the fragrance
of crushed clover, were only a memory that was slowly dissolv-
ing under the drone of traffic, the gray shadows of tall buildings.
Dope was like sleep, and Nadean hoped that if she slept long
enough, she could wake one day to find she had only suffered
through a long, bad dream.

"You just be cool," Jerome told her. "He ain't gonna hurt
you."

Her last fix was wearing off, and already Nadean felt knots
beginning in her stomach. She choked off a sob.

"Give me one more chance, baby," she pleaded. "Please? I'll
work. Do anything you ask."

Jerome slowly shook his head. "Naw, girl. I warned you six
months ago that things had to change. Ain't no free rides in the
city." He leaned and wiped a trickle of tears from her cheek.
"Soon as you done, I'll give you something to make you feel
good." He winked at her while closing the door.

"John" was a white man, mid-forties. Balding. A pudgy gut
spilled over the band of his shorts when he dropped his trousers.
He didn't smile, didn't frown, just stared into her face, then at the
door, the window, back to her face, his eyes wide with fright. He
jiggled his penis in one hand. Nadean moaned, closed her eyes,
and slumped against the mattress.

He pushed her legs apart, mounted her. Through slitted eyelids over his shoulder, Nadean watched his buttocks rise, fall, up and down, up and down, his ass pasty white between her own dark legs. Like a hobby horse—she rode one once in the merry-go-round at the county fair—like a hobby horse. His mouth was hot beside her ear; he hissed, "Cunt. Oh, you black-ass cunt."

The men were identical. They talked the same—voices high with fear and excitement like children doing something wrong—smelled the same, the scent of Aqua Velva mixed with the acrid sweat of terror. A teenaged boy who squealed like a rabbit when Jerome cut his ass and robbed him sounded identical to the old man who wheezed so bad he had to roll off.

Nadean watched the man and woman, the dank hotel room burn in the white-hot coals. "Yeah, that woman long dead," she whispered.

She stayed with the fire until Venus was swallowed by morning glow. Four shimmering beds of coals gushed columns of warm air. Nadean folded the corners of the quilt.

"Hope you 'bout ready to move on, Mister Winter," she said. "Else I'll burn up half the firewood in this county."

Nadean's knees popped when she took a step. "Guess I better get the boy up. Ellis, he ain't gonna follow my road."

Mary and Jeffery rode into Oak Hills on Monday afternoon following a long weekend at the coast. They had spent three nights in a quaint bed and breakfast, complete with a stone fireplace in their room and a bay window perfect for sipping bourbon and watching the changing moods of the sea. Mornings, Mary had risen early, leaving Jeffery to his lingering dreams, and walked alone on the beach under flocks of wheeling gulls.

She was too excited to sleep. Out of impulse, she had applied for a job teaching beginning news writing at the university journalism school. Friday morning, she had received a letter asking that she call the school to schedule an interview.

Mary was reluctant to tell Jeffery. He had recently gotten another promotion, and had hinted twice that now was the time to begin thinking about starting a family. She wished Jeffery weren't so old-fashioned. She knew he liked having her meet him at the door each evening, the smell of dinner spilling from the house. His mother, as well as her own, had dedicated their lives to the home and children. But the years she had spent getting a degree, the possibility of her putting it to use—they would have to talk.

Mary was aggravated by the sight of a spilled trash can beside the street. She sucked in her breath and pointed. "That mess is an eyesore that should not have to be tolerated in this town."

Two weeks ago, Mary had been invited to join the Junior League. Amid the freshness of her morning beach walks, she became more aware of the need for community involvement. Regulating industrial growth, noise pollution, maintaining a clean environment—there were so many areas that conscientious citizens should monitor. Nothing should be allowed that unnecessarily distracted from the good life a person was entitled to.

She thought back to the unhappiness of her childhood. Her father had been an executive for General Motors, a job that required the family to move to another city every couple of years. She remembered with sadness all the big, fine houses they had moved into—every one as sterile as bottled water. And as soon as she did begin to feel at home, had claimed a favorite tree in the backyard to climb, made friends in the private schools she attended, the family would be uprooted and transferred to another freshly painted, odor-free home. She swore her adult life would be different.

Mary had begun to worry that there was too little activism in

Oak Hills. With the rapid growth of the subdivision, the town was expanding at an alarming rate. A new house was begun every week. Without controls, the quiet country life she had opted for might easily be spoiled by an avalanche of low-budget homes, noisy neighbors, or even mobile homes.

"Jeffery, this town needs a community council. A group of people to decide and direct growth. We need an outline established of what we want Oak Hills to look like five, even ten years from now."

Jeffery chuckled. "Calm down." He squeezed her leg. "You always were my little activist."

"Well, things like spilled garbage cans should not be left beside the street. Our little vacation has made me open my eyes a bit to how nice a clean environment really is."

"Well, get busy, Senator. You've got my vote."

When the palm tree swung into view, Mary didn't take it in at once. A cluster of brain cells tickled the back of her mind, hinting that something in the landscape wasn't right. Finally, her eyes accepted the strange shape, snapping wide with astonishment.

Jeffery followed Mary's outstretched arm while slowing the car. Thrusting from the ripped soil on top of Woodrow's hill, he saw the palm arching her long neck southward.

"Well, unless I'm having a flashback from my wilder days," he said matter-of-factly, "that's a palm tree in Woodrow's yard."

Mary leaned across Jeffery and peered through the window as they rolled past. The thing *was* ugly, a starved trunk skinny as a bird's leg, limp fronds hanging like strands of greasy hair, the monstrosity sitting atop a mass of jumbled, orange clay. The mess reminded her of a plane crash, a war scene from *The Sands of Iwo Jima,* one of those ridiculous sets on "The Twilight Zone."

"My God!" she gasped.

□   □   □

Nadean's palm became the new center of conversation in Oak Hills, helping ease the sting of the Tar Heel's defeat in the regional basketball finals. A parade of cars passed by day. By night, people watched the twinkle of fires burning beneath the tree. Opinions were generally divided between the longtime residents of Oak Hills and the newer denizens of the subdivision.

"Might live," one old-timer encouraged. "You know, been years back, but I spit out some orange seeds and one sprouted and grew higher than my head. Took that big freeze in '64 to kill it."

"You got to give it plenty of water," another advised. "That's the key with palm trees. Lots of water needed to make coconuts. I remember when we were fighting on Guam, and when the shooting was low, we'd draw straws and skin up one of them trees and knock down some fruits and . . ."

"Oh, it's a queer-looking thing," said one of the widows, "but you have to admit it's different. I don't believe there's another 'round here, even in Chapel Hill. Not growing. You know, I had this banana tree growing once in a foot tub, and folks would come . . ."

In some ways, the older people viewed the palm with the same awe of their first sight of an airplane tooling across the sky, the hum of a radio, or glimpse of a television screen. It also widened their view of the world.

"Now, I know I'll never get down to Florida, but I can say I've touched a living palm tree."

"Well, what amazes me," another added, "is how God could make trees that are so different. Look at an oak and then at that palm. Reminds me of in the Bible where Jesus is coming into town and they're laying the palm fronds in front of him and . . ."

The mood of many of the subdivision residents changed from initial astonishment into concern or even contempt.

"That man planted the palm merely to draw attention to himself," said a botany professor. "It is impossible for a palm to survive in this climate and soil."

"I think he's doing this just to show off his wealth," another said. "You'd think that in a world where two-thirds of the population is malnourished, a person could find better ways to use their money."

"Well, no matter why he's doing this, that tree is just plain ugly. I'm getting to where I turn my head every time I pass."

Among Mary and Jeffery and their immediate circle of friends, the criticism was not so severe.

"Look, Woodrow is a free spirit," Mary countered. "He always does things different. Let's let him finish this project before we judge."

"That's right," said Dack. "It's obvious he's building some type of theme garden. It'll look better when he's finished."

Mary avowed her faith daily. Woodrow and Nadean were the foundation of her vision of an improved South.

A week passed. Finally, the wilted fronds of the palm began to lift, as if Nadean's vigilance had willed nourishment up the trunk. The yellow pallor ebbed, replaced by a vigorous green, the tips of the fronds searching the points of the compass.

Nadean had continued her night fires for the week, even though the danger of a hard freeze had passed. One twilight as she gathered wood, she stopped at the coo of a dove. The bird's cry was not the echoey song usually drifting from the forest, but louder and closer. Peering overhead, Nadean spied in the palm fronds two doves, one grooming her feathers, the other with his breast full as he began another song.

Nadean stopped piling wood. She went into the house and was soon sleeping soundly.

With the palm out of immediate danger, Woodrow and Ellis were ready to begin construction of the beach. Nadean rested her head against the trunk, closed her eyes, and conjured up an image from childhood.

"I see lots of sand, Woodrow. White like sugar. Mounds of it like cotton candy. And shells in the sand. They been flung up by the water. I see smooth rocks, like the waves been pounding on them for years and years, and I see a flock of them pink birds. The kind that stand on one leg in the water. And that water, it blue as the sky after a storm clears away. That's how it looked in the picture, Woodrow. But, we ought to stop this foolishness now and settle for the palm tree. I know you can't bring the ocean here."

Two days later, a backhoe bit into the cold earth of Woodrow's front yard several feet from the base of the palm. Carefully, Woodrow worked the iron claw, dumping tons of rocky soil to one side. By the end of the day, the hole yawned twice the length of a car and deeper than Woodrow was tall.

"What you digging there in your front yard, Woodrow?" Bill Taylor, the grocer, asked as Woodrow piled his basket of food on the counter. "Your septic tank done quit on you?"

"Pool," Woodrow replied.

"Pool? A swimming pool?"

"Yeah, a beach like in Florida. Gonna haul in some sand and buy some fancy wading birds."

Bill smiled while ringing up the sale. "A pool in the front yard?"

"Yep." Woodrow lumbered from the store. The grocer watched his exit, then spoke to another man sitting close to the kerosene heater.

"Folks can say what they want about that boy, but there ain't another person in this county that has his imagination."

Word circulated among the residents of the subdivision that Woodrow and Nadean were landscaping their yard.

"Those two are so creative," Mary said to Jeffery as they shared a cocktail before dinner. "I get so aggravated at myself for not doing more with our yard." Mary imagined white and pink azaleas lining the drive, tulips growing inside a brick bed, something tasteful and attractive. "I assume they're putting in a large Jacuzzi surrounded by a redwood fence."

"Probably a greenhouse, too, to complement the palm," Jeffery added. "Seems I heard Nadean is interested in exotic plants."

Mary tinkled her ice cubes, wondering how high a fence would have to be to mute the stark image of the palm.

Woodrow shaped the hole to resemble a huge egg, sloping the grade from knee deep at one end to the depth of more than seven feet. The backhoe was returned. Woodrow and Ellis chiseled the walls vertically with shovels.

Next a crew arrived from Raleigh, bringing a blue plastic pool liner that was molded to the contour of the hole, then plumbed with a waterline and drain. After the crew finished, Woodrow and Ellis spent a week mixing concrete in a wheelbarrow and laying a five-foot-wide slab around the edges of the pool. Often as they worked, curious townspeople stopped by to see how work was progressing and offer advice.

Nadean helped where she could. She broke up clods of dirt and raked it smooth, buffed the concrete with a wire brush as it dried, and shooed away curious dogs and cats interested in digging in the piles of fresh earth. She found unbelievable the fact that Woodrow was really building the beach, and dared not hope it could look like the picture in the book. Nothing could be that pretty in real life—could it?

Next, Woodrow and Ellis began shoveling the piles of topsoil and clay, shaping them into gentle slopes similar to dunes bordering a beach. Nadean fussed over each hill, adding more dirt here, raking down another pile. When at last she was satisfied, Woodrow phoned a nearby rock quarry and had them deliver three dump truck loads of the purest white sand they sold. The sand was dumped on the edge of the dunes, Nadean taking the first shovelful and spreading it over the cracked red clay, the granules sliding and sifting and contouring to the earth's form. She spread two more shovelfuls, then removed her shoe and pressed her foot into the damp sand. "It's perfect, Woodrow. Like someone dropped sugar from the sky."

Slowly, over several days, Nadean directed the sculpting of the beach, deciding where each wheelbarrow load was to go, molding with her hands, mounding the sand around the base of the palm, sloping it gently to the water's edge, raking ridges that peaked like sword blades atop each dune. Another truckload was ordered until the base of red clay was buried under at least a foot of sand. Then Nadean scattered the shells she had bought in a crafts shop, turning each to expose its bright belly. She labored under the weight of large, polished rocks Woodrow fetched from the bed of Haw River.

The citizens of Oak Hills watched with either horror or fascination. Ellis became a celebrity at school.

"Hey Ellis, ya'll going to hire some hula girls? What about surfing? You going to learn to surf?"

The jokes were kept in good nature since Ellis's rapid growth over the winter had pushed him to eye level with most boys. They remembered he always had had a fully grown temper. Actually, Ellis thought the entire idea of building a beach was silly, but the excitement it stirred was worth the trouble.

When Nadean was satisfied with every rock, shell, and dune, she studied the pink birds in her mind's eye. They would be the finishing touch, capping the beach like cherries on top of vanilla ice cream.

"They tall and leggy," she told Woodrow. "Sort'a like those white birds you see sometimes hanging around cows in the summer. They got a long, curved bill and like to stand on one leg."

Woodrow screwed up his face in thought. "They ain't chickens?"

"No, crazy. You ever see pink chickens?" Nadean laughed.

"Chickens be running around scratching in the sand and shitting on it."

Ellis searched exotic ads in wildlife and livestock magazines, but found only pheasants, quail, and other game birds for sale. For several days, it seemed the finishing touch to Paradise might go unfound.

Nadean was riding with Woodrow through Durham on their way to buy dog food at the feed mill, when she spied the birds. She squealed and made Woodrow make a U-turn, then jumped out of the cab and ran. The birds stood proudly on one leg in the picture window of a lawn and garden store.

"Thought you wanted live birds," Woodrow said. "These are fake."

"Naw, these be perfect," Nadean said, admiring the brilliant pink, plastic birds, their necks curved as gracefully as a rainbow. "Won't be roosting in the palm, messing in the sand. Won't bite."

She rushed inside. "What the name of those birds in the window?" she asked a startled clerk.

"Flamingos," he answered.

"Flamingos! They flamingos, Woodrow," she shouted. "I'll take a dozen, please."

Nadean stood on the crest of one of the dunes, her eyes closed, studying the picture in her head. It got to be right. Can't mess up now. They look like friendly birds. Like folks in Oak Hills. Like they would stand around in groups and talk.

The plastic birds stood three feet tall with stakes that could be pushed into the ground. Nadean grouped the birds in clusters of three at each rounded corner of the pool. Against the white sand, they stood out like drops of blood.

At dusk, Woodrow turned the valve that began flooding the pool. Under the gathering light of dawn, a tiny ocean appeared, lapping just inches below the white sand beach, the curve of the

palm seen against the sky and reflecting off the smooth water, the
squads of flamingos standing sentinel over a small portion of
heaven.

Mary drew aside the living room drapes to let in the morning.
She watched a startled wren lift on swift wings from the feeder,
followed the bird with her eyes to Woodrow's property line, the
hill—the beach.

"My God!" she gasped. "Jeffery, come here."

The flamingos glinted crimson upon the white sand. Splinters
of sunlight danced off the water and shimmered upon the palm
fronds, the vibrant branches stirred by a light breeze and writhing
like Medusa's hair. The colors and contours seemed even more
bizarre against the ordered backdrop of sweet gums and oaks.

"What's wrong?" Jeffery asked, hurrying into the room. Mary
could only point.

He chuckled. "Ah. Flamingos. A herd of them." He bunched
the fingertips of his right hand toward the ceiling. "The coup de
grace."

"I don't think it is very funny," Mary cried. "I think   I don't
know what to think."

Jeffery moved closer to the window. "I haven't seen plastic
flamingos since I was a kid. There was this little old lady who
lived on our street. She had one on each side of her driveway."

Mary searched the lawn around the beach for any signs that
Woodrow had begun building a fence. Common sense told her a
wall would never hide the palm.

"Jeffery. I have defended Nadean and Woodrow for three
weeks, but this morning, my faith is being sorely tested."

"Don't let it bother you, baby," Jeffery said. "Son of a gun.
Pink flamingos."

Several more times that morning, Mary was drawn to the window. Each time, the sand gleamed whiter, the palm and rocks and plastic birds seemed more ridiculous and out of place. The subdivision heightened the contrast—orderly cedar-sided homes fronted by green, clipped lawns with shrubs and hedges. The new estates blended with the hardwoods, lending a feeling of harmony and permanence, exactly what Mary had longed for all her life. Oh, but that damn beach!

On her fifth trip to the window, Mary spied Nadean standing on one of the dunes, raking the sand with a garden fork. We have got to talk, Mary thought. I'm sure they have a landscaping plan.

Her steps carried her down the drive, the oasis sucking her forward like a vacuum. The flamingos grew tall as horses.

Nadean spied Mary's approach and stopped raking. Mary flashed a brief, tight smile.

"Ain't this something?" Nadean asked. "I been hoping you and Jeffery would come over."

Mary nodded vigorously. "It's something, all right. It is really something."

"Oh, a little more fussing here and there, she be finished. Sure has took some work. Tell me, Mary, how them eagles doing?"

"What eagles?" Mary toed the sand. She blinked, felt woozy, and took a deep breath. "Nadean, when is Woodrow going to build the fence?"

"What fence?"

"The redwood fence. The fence around—around your pool."

Nadean propped against her rake. "Honey, there ain't gonna be no fence. I don't like being closed in by fences."

"But what about your privacy, Nadean? You don't want to bathe and relax in front of the whole community?"

Nadean chuckled. "People want to laugh at this ole body of mine, let them."

No fence! Mary's pulse pounded in her temples. The flamingos grew another foot. She stared at the blue water, trying to stop a sudden sense of vertigo. "Nadean, what I'm trying to say is people just don't build swimming pools in their front yards. They especially don't surround it with sand and big rocks and plastic flamingos. And they certainly—most certainly—do not plant an adult palm tree."

Nadean suddenly resumed her raking. She swept the slope of the dune several times, then stopped and dropped the rake. "Why I want to put a fence up? Keep all this beauty shut off from the world?"

Mary swept her arm in a half circle. "But Nadean, this is so unusual. How many other palm trees and pink flamingos do you see in Oak Hills? None!" Mary stepped forward and clasped her hand on Nadean's shoulder. "Nadean, I like you and Woodrow. That's why I'm saying this to you. People—some people in Oak Hills are upset by this and beginning to say bad things."

Nadean patted Mary's pale arm. "Mary, honey, I thank you for caring 'bout us, but I don't give beans for what people say. The things I been through in my life, all the . . ." Nadean stopped in mid-sentence and looked at the water, then back at Mary. "People talked 'bout me before. Gonna do it again. What can words do to someone like me?"

Mary felt dizzy again. She blinked and stepped back from Nadean. She mumbled a weak goodbye, then retreated for the safety of her green, trimmed lawn.

Mary cornered Alice, the cleaning girl, that afternoon. "Alice," she began, "you've known Woodrow and Nadean for a long time, haven't you?"

"Yes, ma'am. Most of my life."

Mary flipped through the pages of a *McCall's* magazine. "What exactly did Nadean do in Washington? What kind of work?"

Alice busied herself sweeping. Her face colored. "She sold favors," finally the girl answered.

Mary looked up from the magazine. Favors? She imagined a curbside trinket stand. "Favors? What sort of favors?"

Alice stared blankly at Mary. "You know, ma'am. Favors for men. Her—her body."

The magazine slid from Mary's hands to the floor. Mary opened her mouth, but at first no words came out. "What!" she croaked.

"You didn't know?" Alice said, her face twisted with surprise. "Everybody else knows it. The deacons had a closed-door meeting trying to decide what to do." In a lower voice, "There was talk of running her out of town."

Mary, stunned, twisted her wedding band around and around her finger. "And Woodrow just took her in—I mean, I know he's very kind—but he just took her in against everyone's wishes?"

"Well," Alice answered, "most people didn't blame Woodrow much—knowing how his mind is."

Mary blinked. "His mind? How is his mind?"

"You don't know that either?" Alice's embarrassment dissolved under the thrill of spreading gossip. "Ma'am, Woodrow's mind, now that's a long story . . ."

That evening over dinner, Mary told Jeffery of the incredible things she had learned. Jeffery listened in silence until she finished.

"How do you know she was telling the truth?"

"Well, why would she lie? Jeffery, that woman looked at me like I was a simpleton."

"Well, whatever their pasts include, both Woodrow and Nadean seem to be pretty decent people. I don't think we should judge them by things that happened years ago."

"Oh, I know. I fully agree." Mary picked at her food. "But Jeffery, what if we're wrong about them? I mean, all the things happening lately. What if they've been hoodwinking us all along?"

12

"Woodrow, what you say to another party?" Nadean asked as they sat on the front steps, admiring the beach as the sun sank in the western sky. "Can't be no watermelon feast, but we could maybe cook some hot dogs, give folks a chance to come and see what we done here."

Woodrow chewed on a sassafras twig and was silent as he thought. "Reckon we could," he finally said. "A lot of people stopped by to help or give advice. When you thinking of?"

"That's up to you. Weather good, why couldn't we do something Saturday night? My sister got a birthday next week and it would be nice for her."

Woodrow called Ellis from his room and instructed him to make up another batch of signs. Before dusk settled over Oak Hills, word was tacked to light poles and placed in mailboxes that another "do" was on at the Woodrow Bunce place.

"I wish it was summer and everyone could swim at the party," Nadean chattered over supper. "The younguns 'round here would have a fit over that pretty, blue water."

"Ya'll ought to charge admission," Ellis said. "There ain't another pool closer than Chapel Hill."

"Hush such talk," Nadean scolded. "We built that beach for people to enjoy. Not to charge them."

As Woodrow cleaned his plate, he kept glancing at a full moon rising through the tree limbs. His hounds were restless. Forgoing his usual pie and ice cream, Woodrow pushed back his chair and announced he was going out to hunt.

Immediately, Nadean felt her stomach grab. Despite the innocence of his hunts, she still feared the lonely bay of the hounds, the runs dotting her mind with cold flashes of déjà vu. But, she kept her mouth closed. Hadn't he just given her a piece back of her childhood? And anyway, Ellis was here now.

As Woodrow began to dress in his warm clothing, Nadean cleared the table. She worked around Ellis, who was still eating.

"Feed a boy right and he shoot up like a weed," she teased. "Feeding you two like feeding Sherman's army."

Daily, Ellis more resembled a man. A shadow of beard showed on his chin. Nadean had let the hem out of his trousers until the frayed ends showed. Some nights his shins ached from rapid growth, and Nadean would rub them with hot towels smeared with Vick's liniment. Sometimes Ellis read to her from his textbooks, usually tales from history about early explorers, wars, and the civil rights movement. As Nadean stacked the plates, she thought back to a conversation she had had recently with Ellis when he asked her how it felt to be black.

"Black? It don't feel no certain way," Nadean began. "When you were short, that feel any certain way?"

"No, it didn't feel any particular way. But, I got tired of what other people made of it."

"That's what black feels like. Nothing really, 'cept what other people make of it." Nadean pointed at Woodrow sitting in an armchair.

"How it feel to be crazy, Woodrow?" Nadean called.

Woodrow lowered the *Progressive Farmer* magazine he was looking at. "Huh?"

Nadean chuckled. "See. Woodrow, he crazy. You short, and I'm black. And it don't mean shit to a pee pot 'cept what somebody want to make of it."

"I'm not so short now," Ellis said.

"Yeah, that true. And I'm not very black neither. Least I ain't studying what other people say. From now on, I'm just me. You Ellis and that's Woodrow."

Nadean's mind drew back to the present when Woodrow dropped his heavy boots to the floor and sat down to put them on.

Yeah, that's ole Woodrow, she thought, watching him loosen the cords. He a little crazy, and a little like Santa Claus, and a little like the Pied Piper, and a whole lot of something I don't think I'll ever understand.

Jeffery Stewert was usually sleeping by eleven o'clock. He began work at 8 A.M. sharp, his job requiring a rested mind able to meet the stresses of a new day. But tonight he could not sleep. A shakeup was going on in his office, and the next day he had to fire an employee. Jeffery liked the man, but business was business.

Jeffery slipped off the mattress and walked into the bathroom to swallow a couple of aspirins. Might ease the dull drumming above each temple. He washed the pills down with a glass of water, pissed, then walked back to bed, standing over Mary for several seconds watching her sleep. She rested soundly, curled with her back to him, her hip rounding the covers as gently as the green hills curved north of their home. He was careful not to wake her while slipping back under the covers. Mary wore only a T-shirt, and Jeffery felt the heat of one of her buttocks against his thigh. He lay his hand against the soft flesh, remembering once after a party when he had inserted two fingers in her vagina while she slept. Deep in her alcohol sleep, she had only moaned once. The memory embarrassed him, feeling that the intrusion had been unnatural, but it always prompted a strong erection. He wished for a minute she would awaken and want to make love.

Still no sleep. Midnight passed. Jeffery was wondering what neighbor's dog was barking when he heard the first long trumpet of Woodrow's horn. He pushed up against the headboard and listened.

The baying hounds responded to the blast, picking up the volume of the hunt. Jeffery found the sounds not unpleasant, but very lonely, like hearing an owl hoot deep in the woods. He recalled Mary mentioning once that she had heard Woodrow hunting, remembered a neighbor recall a similar sleepless night.

For all the earthiness and simplicity Jeffery admired in Woodrow, there was also something unidentifiable in him that was dreadful. Jeffery had often attempted to name the feeling, but it hung in the reaches of his mind the way a bad dream lingers just out of recall. Jeffery had first felt a shiver on the night of the watermelon feast.

Twilight had fallen, Woodrow standing alone as he had done

most of the afternoon. Jeffery rose from his place on the blanket to walk over and chat. He was only a few yards from Woodrow when he followed the big man's gaze to a satellite crossing the sky. The point of light moved rapidly against the stars, Woodrow watching as solemnly as a statue. Slowly, he thrust his big arm toward the sky, grasping with his fingers as if he wished to pluck the satellite from its orbit. Twice his fingers opened and closed before the point of light disappeared in the earth's shadow. Jeffery was sure he saw the glint of tears in Woodrow's eyes.

What is that emotion, Jeffery wondered? This feeling of chasing something, grasping for it, but it stays just out of reach? What's Woodrow always staring at above people's heads? What's he doing out there running through the woods? I haven't the slightest idea. I know I do have to fire a man tomorrow who has just bought a house, and he hasn't the slightest suspicion either.

Let's see, there's a play we want to see Tuesday night. I got to remember to buy the tickets. We have a dinner date for Saturday night. I need to talk with Mary again about us having a baby.

Life was ordered. Jeffery needed order. His world moved in circles from week to week, planned well in advance so he knew the order of the coming day, the following week, the next month. A man had to have control of his life. None of that stumbling blind through the woods.

In the darkness, a small boy cried out. His mother, quickly wrapping the folds of her housecoat around her waist, hurried to him.

"What's that, Mama?" he asked, grasping her arm when she sat down.

"Shhh, baby, it's all right. That's just a man hunting." She stroked his yellow hair. "Don't be afraid. Those are just hunting dogs you hear. Go back to sleep."

With his mother's hand caressing the nape of his neck, the boy was asleep in seconds. His mother sat quietly listening to his breathing, hearing the hunt sounding off the ridgeline.

The lonely echoes of Woodrow's hunt no longer bothered Nancy Lupo. She was accustomed to the sound, as were most of the longtime residents of Oak Hills. The baying of the hounds, the growl of Woodrow's horn, bothered her less than the lowering of jets as they approached the newly expanded airport outside of Raleigh.

In a strange way, Nancy found the hunt comforting. She had listened to Woodrow since she was a teenager, the sound never changing. Everything else in Oak Hills was changing. Being swallowed up or torn down. People said that soon a single city would stretch from Raleigh to Greensboro, Oak Hills just another of many congested suburbs.

Through the window, Nancy stared at house lights where only months before had stood trees. She remembered the forest, fireflies blinking between the boughs on summer evenings, mushrooms growing in the damp humus, the pretty little trail that led to a grassy knoll overlooking Oak Hills. The hill was now cleared halfway to the crest.

At least Woodrow's hunts were a link to permanence. Nancy had trusted in permanence.

She could still remember so well the day the letter had arrived from the university. She remembered staring at the fat envelope, then tearing into it, holding the letter as gently as a flower. She would be the first in the family to attend college, the first to break away from the routine of Oak Hills. She twirled on the balls of her feet until she was giddy, the letter flapping like a bird's wing.

"Why you want to spend all that time, Lord, not to mention the money, when you can have a good life right here?" her mother asked.

"I want to see places, Mama. I want to be a nurse in a big city hospital. Maybe even a doctor."

"Honey, I'm afraid for you to go running off like that. You're liable to get up there around all those wild northern students and learn no telling what."

Nancy's father had less to say. "You want to go, we'll find the money. Maybe put a second mortgage on the house. But baby, I had sort of hoped you would become a beautician like your mother. We'd see more of you."

Mack, her boyfriend of four years, sulked when he was told. "And what about us? You're just going to run off to college and forget about our plans?"

"But, Mack. I'll be home nearly every weekend. Nothing will change between us. I promise."

But, by the way Mack looked off into the branches of a tree, slowly breaking a stick into shorter and shorter lengths, Nancy knew if she left their plans would change.

Instead of attending freshman orientation that August, Nancy and Mack were married. They went to Myrtle Beach for three days. The baby was born eleven months later. Nancy earned her license from the technical school and began tending a chair in her mother's salon. She told herself she had been silly to dream so extravagantly. Oak Hills was home. Permanence was important—a way of living a person could depend on year to year.

The hounds crested a hill, their bays ringing like hammers. The boy whimpered so Nancy caressed his cheek. Mack said Woodrow's hunts were just more of his craziness. He never killed anything, didn't even carry a gun. Nancy tried to imagine how Woodrow must look as he ran after his dogs, lumbering in pursuit of God knows what. Pure craziness? She had stifled her own craziness at eighteen in exchange for permanence.

Nancy curled ringlets of her son's hair. "Sleep, baby," she whispered. She wished she were sleeping, and out of reach of her thoughts.

Mack was drinking too much. The family farm never had cleared much money, and every year she feared it would go under. Somehow, Mack always came up with the mortgage. So many of their neighbors were new, from out of state, had college degrees, had their hair fixed in Chapel Hill.

Lately, the smell of wet hair was making Nancy sick. She feared she was pregnant again. The acceptance letter was folded in her jewelry box, but she never looked at it now. The fireflies were long gone.

Nadean listened to the ebb and surge of the hunt while sewing in a rocking chair in front of the fireplace. Through Ellis's partially open bedroom door, she heard his light nasal snoring, and did not feel as lonely as usual when Woodrow hunted. The baying hounds bothered her no more than any whippoorwill cry, hoot owl, or creaking floor—those sounds that reminded people in the deep of night that they grew older each day and nearer to death.

Nadean glanced at the clock and saw that midnight had passed. The hunt had swung and was following the twisting path of Haw River. She put down her work, yawned, and walked to the front door. She turned on the porch light and walked outside into the cold to once again read the thermometer nailed to the wall. Thirty-one degrees. Wasn't too bad. The man from the plant school at the university had said that heat wasn't needed unless the cold dropped below twenty.

Beyond the porch light, Nadean studied the beach. The bright shells, flamingos, and rocks glinted in the light. The palm curved above the water. Nadean felt the tree no longer looked out of place, but rested against the horizon as gently as any sycamore or gum.

Why can't a palm tree grow in Oak Hills, she thought? I'm growing, feeling the best I feel in years. Ellis, he finally growing now he's with Woodrow. Something about this hill we live on make a person sprout like a weed and shine. Something magic.

Nadean looked into the fronds. You part of the family now, honey. We got a strange mixture on this hill, but it's home. My mama told me once there weren't no such thing as home, but now I know better.

"Them poor-ass niggers be talking 'bout you for a month," Jerome said as he eased down the pitted dirt lane from the tobacco barn. In the rearview mirror he saw everyone watching. Beside the fenders raced several small, shouting boys.

Nadean tugged at the hem of her dress. Already she wished she hadn't talked Jerome into swinging by Oak Hills. At least not like this.

"Yeah, they'll talk," Nadean whispered, "but talk ain't shit."

"I thought a couple of them dudes would shit," Jerome said. "Shit right in their pants. Who them white men?"

"Bunce brothers. They own half the county."

"Who was that big motherfucker? Looked like he had just dropped his candy bar."

Nadean laughed. "You must be talking 'bout Woodrow. He's all right. Least he'll say hello. Woodrow kind'a simpleminded. People say he always been that way."

Once on blacktop, Jerome eased down on the gas, leaving the children. One threw a rock, but it fell short. A dog raced the front tire, snapping at the blur of white letters. Nadean reached into the glove compartment, peeled back one edge of the liner, and pulled out a joint. The good smoke eased her back from the seat's edge.

The home land passed—fields, patches of hardwood, houses with neatly trimmed yards. The air was hot and wet, thunderstorm weather. A red-tailed hawk floated high above a plowed field on a thermal.

Ain't changed none, Nadean thought. Not a bit in these past years. Home always be home, even if you gone for seventy years.

Jerome nodded toward the joint. "You better go easy on that shit. You'll be talking trash to your mama."

Nadean took another deep drag from the joint, then held it out for Jerome. He shook his head. Her lungs burned, but she kept the smoke down.

Blacktop ended. Nadean pointed to the left fork of a clay road. She rolled down the glass, sniffing the dust from the tires, the musk of freshly mowed fescue, tiny wild roses wound through a fence of hog wire. Home's heart drew closer, a rambling, unpainted frame house with wide porches.

Nadean sucked in a deep breath of the hot air. "You laugh when we get there, I'll cut you." She smiled, but was very serious.

Jerome lifted his fingers from the steering wheel and spread them. "Laugh? Didn't I tell you how I grew up? Ain't nothing to laugh at over a person being poor."

The engine of the Lincoln grumbled as Jerome slowed down, then swung into the wide front yard.

Home eternal. Two mongrel dogs raced barking down the steps, their tails wagging faster than their mouths. The clay yard was raked clean, flower beds surrounded by rings of stones, a blackened, three-legged wash kettle squatting over old cinders. In the front window, an electric fan rattled, pushing the vinyl curtain against the screen. The hot air emptying from the house was thick with the odor of collards being cooked with fatback. Three small children stood on the porch, staring with wide eyes, the youngest boy naked from his waist down. He turned and ran for the screen door. The tallest child shouted for the dogs to hush.

Screen door slowly opened. Who is that out there? Wide female face, tufts of hair licking from under a scarf. Young woman. She begins shouting, "She's here. She's here. She here now."

The old woman carried a dishrag. She wound it into a knot, standing straight and skinny at the top of the steps, her hair nearly gray but shiny and combed. Nadean began sobbing.

"Not too long, hear?" Jerome said. "Atlanta still five hours."

Through her tears, home danced in splintered colors—dog spinning for his tail, curious rooster pecking at a tire, fan blades whirling, naked child peeking through his mama's legs, one step, jump one, long step, Nadean hugged the thin woman to her bosom.

"Mama, I'm home."

Dog sniffing Nadean's perfumed ankle. Quiet, except for the rattling fan. The old woman's back was stiff, cordy like strands of small rope. Nadean smelled the collard steam on her mother's neck. Slowly, the old woman's arms lifted, tightened around the young woman's waist, smoothed the material of her dress like stroking a baby's cheek, then hugged with the need of years.

"Baby, that really you? You're a woman now. Nadean, that really you?"

They sobbed, rocking back and forth. The dog whined for attention. Jerome left his car and walked down the road to a shady patch of woods.

Nadean ate from a plate of collards, nibbled corn bread, sipped from a mason jar filled with cold, sweet tea.

"He can't come in even for a drink?" Essie asked. "Hot as it is out there?"

"Mama, he don't mean bad by it. He just that way," Nadean answered. "Jerome uncomfortable around people he don't know."

"We ain't hiding nothing," Essie said. "He have things he don't want people knowing?"

"No, Mama."

Essie's back was straight again and cordy. The more they talked, the harder it was for her to hide her anger. "Reckon he don't like telephones, neither. These long years and not once you called to let me know you were still breathing."

The collards were beginning to taste like wax. Nadean laid her fork on the table. "It wasn't his fault, Mama. A hundred times I started to call. I'd pick it up, then put it back down. Jerome, he's a good man. Went out of his way to bring me here."

"I got my ideas 'bout Jerome. Got you dressed like something off the street. I ain't seen yet what you call a good man."

Nadean swirled the ice in her jar. A fly bothered her, buzzing around her head. It a mistake coming, even after all this time. She still don't listen.

"Mama, this dress, that's what people wear in D.C. Jerome, he's helping me. He's making me into somebody."

"And we ain't somebody? You weren't somebody 'fore you left? I ain't noticed no ring on your finger. Looks to me like Jerome helping himself."

Nadean shooed the fly. It joined several others perched on a light bulb. Ain't never seen no ring on your finger, neither, she wanted to say, but stifled the words.

Essie shooed the children away from the screen door. She wound the dishrag, unwound it, observing Jerome as he squatted in the shade of a cottonwood tree. She sighed. "I know he's sweet. Sweet as new apple juice. The good Lord knows how many times I bit into one of them apples. But, the sweetness in them don't last long. 'Fore you know it, that juice turn to wine and have your head all messed up, and then if you not real careful, it goes sour as vinegar."

Essie tossed her rag into a bucket of water in the sink. She walked behind her daughter, leaned and massaged her bare brown shoulders. Nadean trailed one hand across her breasts and rested it atop her mother's hand. Strong hands, stronger they seemed than any man's. Long, nimble fingers that could wring the head off a rooster or wipe the snot from a child's lip. Nadean traced her fingertips across the smooth, cool skin.

"I reckon I'm too hard on you, baby," Essie said. "Reckon I weren't no example for you. Don't know where one of them men be today. I just want it better for you."

Nadean turned in her chair, grasping her mother's hands. "It's gonna be different, Mama. I don't even like D.C. much. Too much noise and people. Oftentime, I think of coming back home after I save some money. Me and Jerome could buy a place, settle down, and have a family. Mama, I think about that a lot. This here is home."

Essie's eyes glistened. Wrinkles creased her cheeks when she smiled. "You, them poor little white younguns in the boys' home, every dog I see throwed out 'side the road—looking for the same thing. Think there something called home out there, maybe 'round the next curve. Baby, home ain't nothing more than where you work, where you get old and stiff. Where you end up dying. That happen just as quick in D.C."

Outside, the heavy door of the Lincoln slammed. Twice, the horn tooted. Essie cupped her daughter's hands between hers.

"You get in that car and ride, girl. Don't dwell on coming back to something that ain't here. This place drying up like a scab. I could, I'd leave running."

The horn tooted again. The fly buzzed. Through the screen, a child begged for a cup of water.

Nadean shivered and drew her shawl closer around her shoulders. She glanced once more at the thermometer to make sure the air wasn't too cold. "No, Mama," she whispered. "You were right about most things, 'cept one. We don't tote home around with us and set it up where we please like something out of a bag. Home stays in just two places—on the land where you were raised, and always, always in the back of your mind."

Saturday dawned with a bright sun and warm March wind out of the south. Nadean was so excited about the party, she was up before light, cooking breakfast, then shooing Woodrow and a grumbling Ellis from bed.

"Ellis, you sleep your life away if I wasn't around to boot you in the rear," Nadean teased. "You look out that front door, you'll see the first true day-a-spring."

"Come on, Woodrow," she continued. "Pour some coffee in your belly and fire up. We got a party to get ready for." She shoveled scrambled eggs and grits on his plate, beside buttered toast and link sausage.

Party fare would be hot dogs, burgers, chips, and beer. Nadean had told Ellis to write "Bring a Side Dish" on the last line of his signs, so that plenty of eating was ensured. Woodrow borrowed a large gas grill from the community center, then drove into Chapel Hill to buy a keg while Ellis and Nadean lugged home several sacks of food. By mid-afternoon, blue flames were heating the grill, a keg of Blue Ribbon was chilling in a tub filled with ice. A trickle of guests began to climb the hill, all eyes gazing with fascination at the bright colors of Nadean's inland beach.

"Five more minutes, darling," Jeffery told Mary from where he shaved at the bathroom sink. Mary lay stark naked under a sheet in the middle of bed, her buttocks resting on a pillow that tilted her pelvis upward. Like everything Jeffery did, he was meticulous and ordered in their plan to get pregnant, seeding her every three days so his sperm count would be populous and young. They had decided that a son should come first. Jeffery had read that male sperm cells were faster swimmers but quicker to tire, thus the pillow to give them a gravitational boost in their race for the egg.

Mary stared at the ceiling, feeling loose and relaxed after sex, but a bit indignant over being treated like a brood mare. She heard car doors slamming in the direction of Woodrow's house and figured the party was beginning and that she needed to get off her back and start dressing. "How much longer, honey?" Mary called.

"Thirty seconds," came his reply.

Mary took a deep breath. She was still upset over Nadean's beach, but felt certain Nadean was not serious about leaving the pool and sand exposed to the community. She had talked with several of her neighbors, who shared her concern, and they had agreed to tactfully suggest several ways of fencing the beach that would be attractive, while helping it blend in with the architecture of the surrounding homes. Certainly Nadean would listen.

"Time," Jeffery called. He appeared in the bathroom door, smiling at her, his freshly shaven face spotted with flecks of shaving cream. "Bet you a dollar you're with child."

Mary scooted off the pillow and slipped into her underwear. Through the window, she saw more than a couple dozen people already gathered at Woodrow's. Smoke rose from a large grill. She observed the cloudless sky, wondering what Shelby and Fran were wearing, then decided on jeans and a light sweater. Last, she topped her head with a Panama hat a girlfriend had brought her from Central America.

"Don't jiggle it too much," Mary warned Jeffery as they climbed the hill. Jeffery carried a covered dish that contained a molded gelatin vegetable salad. Mary slowed as they neared the beach, the colors sharp under a bright sun. She spied Nadean and Woodrow standing together at the edge of the crowd.

"Hello, Nadean, Woodrow," Mary said, kissing each on the cheek. Jeffery smiled and nodded and apologized that he couldn't shake hands.

Mary lifted the lid. "I hope you like gelatin salad," she said. "I thought it would go well with the franks."

Nadean and Woodrow stared hard at the quivering, green mound, bits of tomato, celery, carrot, and green pepper suspended inside. "That sure is pretty," Nadean said, her forehead wrinkled in wonder. "Jeffery, you can put it over there on one of them picnic tables."

"Well," Mary said, clasping her hands together and smiling at Woodrow. "You two have been the busy bees these last weeks." She swept her hand in a half arch.

"Kind'a late, but it's for her birthday," Woodrow said.

"Well, wherever did you get the idea?" Mary asked, her voice going shrill at the end. "I mean, it's so unusual."

Nadean took Woodrow's hand. "From Woodrow pulling the youngun out of me. I told him I liked the beach, and next thing I know, here come a palm tree down the main fare of Oak Hills."

Woodrow rocked his weight from foot to foot, embarrassed by the attention. Jeffery returned to the group. "I like this," he said. "I was telling Mary that I hadn't seen flamingos like these since I was a kid."

Mary gave her husband a hard look. "Well, I will say," she began, "that there are several ways you could accent the pool so nicely. Redwood or cedar would be beautiful." Mary glanced at Nadean, whose smooth face showed no hint that she even remembered their conversation about a fence.

"We just want folks to enjoy it," Nadean said. "Soon as it gets warm, ya'll welcome anytime to come and swim."

The party grew steadily. A curious mixture of side dishes filled the two picnic tables as the natives of Oak Hills and the subdivision people converged: deviled eggs, quiche lorraine, green beans with smoked pork, Boston baked beans, stewed cabbage, sauerkraut with sausage, collard greens, kohlrabi, corn boiled on the cob, corn creole, fried onion rings, whole onions stewed in wine, cabbage and carrot slaw, gelatin salads, the good smell of franks and burgers wafting over the beach as they began to sizzle on the hot grill.

Ellis turned the franks regularly so they wouldn't burn and studied people gathered in small groups. He was disappointed that the bus from the Home hadn't arrived, but doubted that it would. Enzor was tightly controlled by the Methodist deacons, the core of a group of Oak Hills residents who still balked at accepting Woodrow and Nadean's relationship. He also noticed that fewer of the subdivision people were attending. Folks seemed awkward and controlled, as if intimidated by the towering palm. Ellis hoped that as dusk gathered and drinking increased, things would liven up.

Ellis sipped on his first glass of beer. What the hell, he was his own boss now. Earlier, he had walked over to the keg and poured himself a draft, no one seeming to pay him any mind. The beer was cold and bitter and not as good as he had hoped. He held his nose and gulped, a numbness beginning at the center of his forehead.

Ellis waved people to the grill when the franks had begun to split. Plates were filled, most people choosing the side dishes they were accustomed to. Nadean helped herself to a section of Mary's gelatin salad, but had to make herself eat it under Mary's gaze. She was glad when she saw her sister's car, followed by two others, pull up and stop in front of their yard. Children spilled from the doors, followed by Jackie, her husband, and several black men and women that Nadean didn't recognize.

"Hey, girl," Nadean said, meeting her sister halfway up the lawn and hugging her. "I was starting to think ya'll weren't coming."

"We just slow," Jackie answered. "And the traffic is so bad in Durham." She looked over Nadean's shoulder at the palm. "Lord, Nadean. I never seen nothing like that. Looks like something in a magazine." She waved her husband forward. "You ever seen anything so pretty?" she asked him.

Jackie introduced the other adults to Nadean, all residents of the city housing project where they had moved. One of the men stared intently at Nadean, his eyes moving up and down.

"Ya'll come on up and eat," Nadean said, walking them up the hill. "There's plenty." She introduced the new people to Woodrow.

Dusk settled over Oak Hills. Woodrow lit several Coleman gas lamps. People mingled better now, the keg flowing well, some people sipping from their private caches of whiskey or wine. Nadean had moved away from a group and was standing alone when the man who had stared so hard at her appeared at her elbow.

"You looking fine tonight, sug," he said, staring into Nadean's eyes. "Lady like you shouldn't have to stand alone."

"Oh, you don't have to worry 'bout me getting lonely," Nadean answered. "I'm so busy looking after things, I can hardly slow down."

"Somebody ought to be looking after you," he said, his eyes moving down her body again. "If you were my woman, you wouldn't be lifting a finger out here."

Nadean felt the man place his hand on the small of her back. Embarrassed, she hesitated a second, then chuckled and moved his hand. "Don't worry 'bout me. I get taken care of plenty." She looked for Woodrow and spied him talking with several locals across the beach.

The man put his hand on her again, this time squeezing her ass. Nadean's dormant street instincts surprised her, and without pause, she slapped his arm hard and twisted away. "You liable to lose that hand," she hissed.

His eyes widened with surprise, then narrowed in anger. "Why you selling out, babe? You love money that good?"

"What the hell you mean?"

"Why a good-looking thing like you living with some old crazy-ass honky, less it's for money. He must pay you real good."

"The hell with you, nigger," Nadean said and turned away, her face burning. She walked straight toward Woodrow, intending to tell him, then decided better. She took a deep breath and walked up quietly behind the big man.

"Naw, that ain't it," she heard Woodrow saying to one of the men. His words were extra slow, the way he talked when embarrassed.

"Shit, Woodrow," the man kidded, "I bet she's so hot, you have to carry a bucket of water to bed just in case things get out of hand." The other men laughed. Woodrow stammered as he tried to speak.

Nadean slinked backward from the group of men, a pain flickering between her temples. She decided to walk to the house for an aspirin and a quiet place to think. She was nearly to the porch when she heard a splash, then shouting.

Mary was talking to Shelby and Fran about how to approach Nadean, when several children raced past, shouting and slapping their legs as if riding horses. The leader cut around another group of adults, skirted the edge of the pool, tripped on one of Nadean's colorful rocks, and fell headlong into the deep end of the water.

A scramble ensued as the boy shouted once and went under. Several women screamed for help, a couple of the men tugged frantically at their shoes. Claudia Maxwell, a high school senior and member of the swimming team, hit the water fully clothed and came up with the struggling child held in the crook of her arm. Folks crowded the edge of the pool and shouted encouragement as she paddled to the side. Woodrow bent and grasped Claudia's shoulders and pulled her and the boy to dry ground in one motion.

"Give him room," Claudia shouted, as the boy spit and coughed. His father, Mack Lupo, pushed through the crowd and bent over him. He slapped his son's back, scolding him the whole time.

"I told you twice not to be running. You're getting a spanking when you get home."

The boy began shivering in the chill night air, a sob swelled from his throat. His mother knelt and hugged the boy, placing her sweater around his shoulders. Another man stepped forward and kneeled before the boy. He roughly shoved Mack aside. "This ain't no time to lecture him," the man said. "He needs to go to the emergency room for observation. He might have gotten water in his lungs."

Mack stared at his dislodged hand, then at the man. "And just who the hell are you telling me what to do about my boy?"

"My name is Derrick Lawson and I'm a physical therapist. Fluid in the lungs can lead to pneumonia."

"Well, I tell you what, Derrick," Mack said, rising to his feet. "Shoving my hand can get your nose broke, too. All he got was some water in his throat."

Derrick stood and faced Mack. "I'm just trying to help. He should be examined by a doctor."

"I bet you live in the subdivision," Mack said. He had drunk a lot of beer, his temper already strained after hearing several days ago that the hills above town were wanted for development—a sure end to the only cash crop he'd had any luck with these last few years.

"I do," Derrick answered.

"Figured it, big as your mouth is. Let me tell you something, buddy. I'm sick of you Yankees and California hippies moving in here, then trying to run everything."

Nancy tugged at her husband's arm. "Let's get Tommy home and into some dry clothes," she urged.

Derrick held up one arm. "I was just trying to help, mister. If he was my son, I'd care more."

Mack shoved the man backwards. A murmur rolled through

the crowd. "I'm sick of you people, hear me? Ya'll come in here
building your fancy houses and taking all the land, and now you
stand there and tell me I don't care about my boy."

Mack tried to shove the man again, but Derrick was quicker,
had played lacrosse at Colgate, and was anticipating him. He
shoved back so hard that Mack stumbled backwards and would
have gone down if he hadn't fallen against the trunk of the palm.
When he straightened, he shook his head, then bent and lifted an
empty wine bottle from the sand. When his wife grabbed his arm,
he shoved her aside. "Come on, buddy," Mack said, waving the
bottle. "Shove me again."

Woodrow stepped between the men then. "Don't," he said.
"Put it down, Mack."

Mack stared at Woodrow, his face sliding into a sneer. "Who's
side you on anyway, Woodrow? Bank's, I guess. Ya'll Bunces
hadn't started selling land, none of this would ever have happened."

Woodrow stepped forward slowly until he was close enough
to reach and take the bottle. Mack stared blankly at the crowd,
then turned and lifted his son and stomped for his truck, his wife
following. Within an hour, every other guest had found reason
to go home.

Nadean helped Woodrow pick up trash from the beach after
everyone had left. Ellis was in the house, hugging the toilet with
the dry heaves. Nadean's mind whirled, her stomach sour. Everything had gone so wrong, when all she had wanted was for folks
to talk and laugh like they did at the watermelon feast, to enjoy
her and Woodrow's hard labor.

The white sand was stained with spilled wine, littered with
scraps of hot dog and cigarette butts. Paper cups and two soggy
buns floated in the water. Nadean found beneath the palm what
looked like a small green ball. She picked it up and turned it in

her hand. "Must'a fallen when that man hit the tree," she told
Woodrow. She cradled a tiny green coconut.

Mary needed two Valiums to get to sleep, but still awoke at
daybreak, the palm tree centered in her mind. By the time Jeffery
joined her at the breakfast table, she was on her third cup of Earl
Grey tea.

"I just can't get over last night," she began. "Things keep
playing over and over in my head like a movie."

Jeffery poured himself tea. "Well, it was quite a scene. Not the
sort of thing you'd expect in this neighborhood."

"Well, that's just it," Mary continued. "The man trying to
fight Derrick wasn't from here. At least, not from Whispering
Pines."

"It's best forgotten," Jeffery said. "You find hotheads in about
every group."

"I can't forget it, Jeffery," Mary said shrilly. "It's all I've
thought about all night. Not just the fight. That pool is not only
ugly, it's dangerous."

Jeffery took a seat. Mary watched him spoon sugar into his tea.
"Jeffery, I'm very upset with Woodrow and Nadean. It was
enough of a shock finding out about their true pasts, but now I'm
beginning to think they are just two seedy, low-class people who
took advantage of our hospitality and friendship."

Jeffery carefully measured his sugar. "We never asked them
directly about their past, honey. We listened to rumors and assumed a lot of things."

"But they should have been honest up front," Mary argued.
"We're liberal people. Jeffery, they were intentionally lying to
us."

"Okay. We'll keep our distance from now on," Jeffery answered. "It's as simple as that."

"No, it's not that simple, honey. Haven't you taken a really good look at that . . . pool? It's the most horrid thing I've ever seen. It spoils the peace of the entire community. People have rights. They shouldn't have to look at a garbage heap through their window."

"All right! I'm convinced." He took a long sip from his cup.

Mary recoiled. "Well, you don't have to act so perturbed."

"I'm not perturbed," Jeffery said. "I just don't want to discuss this right now. It's breakfast time and all week at work I had to listen to problems."

"Jeffery. You don't understand. We defended these people. Now they're mocking us."

"Okay. Get up a petition. Call the police. I don't know. I'm sure there are laws governing this sort of thing."

Jeffery retreated behind the sports pages of the newspaper. Mary retreated to the kitchen, her feelings hurt, and began setting the table, plates clinking heavily against the polished cherry wood.

Maybe the townspeople were right all along, Mary mused. Maybe Woodrow and Nadean intended trouble right from the start? Well, I intend to confront them. They're not going to spoil our community. Together, people can demand their rights.

Three nights later, Mary headed a meeting of fifteen residents of the subdivision.

"I've called this meeting to discuss a matter that disturbs me, and I feel certain must also disturb you," Mary said. "I'm speaking of the mess that Woodrow Bunce has created on his front lawn."

A chorus of mumbles rose from the listeners.

"Now, I don't claim to be an expert, but I do know people have rights concerning what a neighbor can do with his or her property. What Mr. Bunce has done is not only an eyesore, but is a danger to young children. It could also possibly devalue surrounding property."

A stronger mumble rolled through the crowd. "What are you proposing?" someone asked.

"Well, I'm not sure, but I know something has to be done. Like I've told some of you, Bunce has a long history of psychotic behavior. He could go on God-knows-what tangent next."

Peter Wilkins raised his hand. "I heard a rumor today that Bunce is considering raising hogs on his back property."

Mary shuddered. The crunch of wheat crackers and Brie stopped.

"As I said," Mary continued, "anything could happen next. We are all intelligent people. We are activists. Let's pool our minds and think."

Opinions ranged on how to approach the problem. A few people even argued that Woodrow was within his rights, but were slowly swayed as Mary filled them in on Nadean and Woodrow's history.

"I am so shocked I could die!" exclaimed one woman. "All this time I thought Nadean to be such a gentle person."

"Hey, I thought Woodrow was the salt of the earth," another said.

The white wine flowed, the Brie softened and gushed. Plots were debated.

"Well, my tendency is to live and let live," Shelby said, "but a community has to be a fit place to raise a family." In a lowered voice, "I heard from a reliable source that the young man living with Bunce was kicked out of the boys' home. Can you imagine what goes on between a delinquent, a mental case, and a prostitute?"

By the bottom of the third bottle of wine, a decision had been reached to form a community council. Mary was elected chairperson. A petition would be circulated asking that Woodrow remove the palm and erect a minimal six-foot fence around his pool. A committee was formed to begin studying means of installing a building code in Oak Hills that would ensure all future construction was acceptable to a family-orientated community.

Mary and Jeffery shared a nightcap after the last neighbor left.

"I'd like to say, I'm quite impressed with the way you've taken charge," Jeffery said. "I'm seeing a new side of you."

"Well, I will admit I have a tendency to be sometimes a little naive," she answered. "But when my home is being trampled on, I can get pretty aroused."

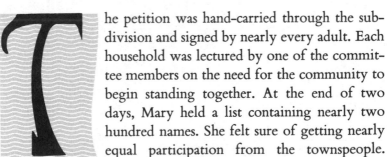

he petition was hand-carried through the subdivision and signed by nearly every adult. Each household was lectured by one of the committee members on the need for the community to begin standing together. At the end of two days, Mary held a list containing nearly two hundred names. She felt sure of getting nearly equal participation from the townspeople. After all, they had seen through Woodrow and Nadean's scam from the beginning. She began at Bob Garner's Florist.

"I think you will want to add your name to this petition, Mr.

Garner," Mary said. "We are simply asking that Woodrow Bunce show a little respect toward the other residents of this fine community."

"Yeah?" Garner said. He took the sheet of paper, raised his glasses off the bulb of his nose, and began reading. "Don't believe I know a single name here," he said finally. " 'Cept you."

"Oh, I can assure you they're all neighbors. I began by signing people in the subdivision."

Garner nodded, reading over the names again. He had once hoped that the subdivision would be a boon to his business. Time had proven him wrong. Nearly all the new residents worked in either Chapel Hill, Raleigh, or the Research Triangle, and shopped the fancier boutiques there. Except for an occasional emergency bouquet or table arrangement, his customers remained the people whose anniversaries and birthdays he remembered by heart.

Garner reread the opening paragraph of the petition. "So, now. This paper is asking that Woodrow cut down that palm tree?"

"Yes, and clean up his front yard, or at least, contain it inside a wall."

Garner twisted the corner of his mustache. Earlier that day, Nadean had stopped by to order azalea bushes she planned to plant in a circle around the beach. Slowly, he had discovered he liked Nadean's shy ways and soft words. He also had found he liked to watch the flutter of the palm fronds when the wind blew, liked the contrast of the white sand and blue water. The scene reminded him of the good two years he had spent at Pearl following the war.

And Woodrow *was* a damn nut. No denying that. But you had to like the boy. There wasn't a mean bone in him. He was honest, and therefore carried no more guilt for his actions than a child. What did these new people have against the beach, anyway? Garner liked bright things. He had worn checked trousers for years after they went out of style. Over his mantel at home was a picture of Jesus on the cross painted on crushed velvet. He had long planned one day to build a fish pool in his own front yard, complete with lily pads, guppies, and concrete frogs.

"I believe I'll pass on signing this, Mrs. Stewert," Garner said. He handed Mary the paper. "That palm tree doesn't bother me, ma'am."

"It's not just the palm tree," Mary exclaimed. "What about those plastic flamingos and mounds of sand? There is even talk that he is going to start growing pigs."

Garner chuckled. "That's *raising* pigs, ma'am."

Mary flushed. "Don't you care what is happening to your community, Mr. Garner?"

The chuckle froze in Garner's throat. He felt a flicker of anger burn his cheeks. "Oh, yes, ma'am, I care."

He remembered when lush fields and stands of hardwood surrounded Oak Hills. He remembered shooting squirrels from oak tops, remembered felling an eight-point buck from his own backyard. A creek filled with bullfrogs and trout had flowed where the subdivision now stood.

"Yes, Mrs. Stewert, I care very much about this community and would like to see a lot of things changed. But believe me, that palm ain't what bothers me."

Mary found that Garner's attitude was typical of most longtime residents. They offered varying excuses for not signing—too busy, didn't want to get involved, wanted to think about it longer—but declined to add their names.

"I find it completely baffling," Mary told Jeffery that night. "These same people were close to forming a lynching party when Nadean moved in, and now they defend her. It's crazy."

"Country people are different, baby. They take longer to think and make up their minds. Just be patient."

"Jeffery, we are country people, too. We live just as far from Chapel Hill as anyone here. We have the same ideals, even if we weren't raised in Oak Hills."

The committee decided to present the petition to Woodrow and Nadean the next day, regardless of the lack of full support.

Nadean sensed trouble when she saw Mary's car stop in front of the house. She had neglected to tell Woodrow of their earlier conversation, and now here came Mary and another young woman walking with brisk steps up the hill. Nadean dropped the dishrag she held and walked from the sink to the front porch.

Mary nodded briskly from the yard. "Good afternoon. Is Mr. Bunce home?"

"Woodrow? Yeah, he in the living room." Nadean turned and called for him. "Ya'll want to come in?"

Mary shook her head. "No, thank you. We're in a hurry." Between her hands she held tightly a manila folder.

Nadean smiled at the other woman, who immediately dropped her eyes. She remembered her from one of the dinner parties last fall. One of the eagle ladies.

Woodrow swung open the front door. "Afternoon."

Again, Mary nodded briskly, then opened the manila folder and removed two sheets of typing paper that had been stapled together. She cleared her throat. "Mr. Bunce, in no way do we wish to embarrass you or Nadean, but the community is upset over what you have done to your front yard."

"Done what?" Woodrow asked.

Mary fluttered one hand, half turning toward the beach. "That. The palm tree. The sand and rocks. Those birds. That is not something one puts in public view."

"You don't?" Woodrow's eyebrows went up.

"Yeah, why don't you?" Nadean echoed.

Mary ignored the questions. She reached out her arm, the papers quivering between her fingers. "Mr. Bunce, this is a copy of a petition containing the names of two hundred and three people in Oak Hills who are upset over your yard. We are asking that you remove the palm tree and install a proper fence around your pool."

Woodrow combed his hair with his fingers while scanning the list of names. "I don't see hardly five people here I know."

"Everyone on the list is one of your neighbors, I can assure you."

Nadean's initial shock was rapidly boiling over into anger. "What you mean remove the tree? Tree ain't got wheels on it, ya know."

"Cut it down. Dig it up."

"Huh! And what you talking about a fence? We ain't cows."

Mary drew a deep breath. "Nadean, I have checked with the county, and it is illegal to have an unfenced pool. It's dangerous for small children. You remember what happened the other night?"

Nadean blinked several times, then looked at Woodrow. "Well, we sure don't want nobody getting hurt, do we, Woodrow?" Nadean's eyes brightened with a thought. "We could get some of that hog wire rolled up in the shed and some cedar posts. Woodrow, he could build a fence that a bull couldn't get through, but still would let people see inside."

Mary's face was red. Her voice was drawing high and forced. Her companion kept shifting her weight from one foot to the other. "I don't even want to know what 'hog wire' is, but I do know this. Your yard is an eyesore," Mary forced out. "It doesn't fit the neighborhood. You need a high fence, Nadean, something that keeps people from seeing inside. I thought you might understand without such harsh words."

"Well, I sure to hell don't," Nadean answered. "An eyesore! Hard as me and Woodrow and Ellis worked, you calling it ugly?" Nadean's anger flowed down her spine, put a tremble in her knees. "What if we don't want to cut down that tree? Or build a fence?"

"Then we will be forced to take further steps," Mary answered. "There are laws."

"Laws, balls." Nadean ripped the paper from Woodrow's hand and crumpled it. "There ain't no law that tells a man what he can make on his own land, is there, Woodrow?"

Woodrow didn't answer. His eyes were on the horizon again. "Naw, there ain't no such a law," Nadean answered for him. "Best thing I see, ya'll ought to haul your fancy behinds on down that hill and leave. Tell folks they don't have to look up here if they don't like the view."

Nadean tossed the ball of paper on the floor. Mary took a step back.

"You'll hear from us again," Mary said. "We were trying to approach the problem in a nice way."

"Well, hearing better be a bullet if you 'spect me to cut down that tree. Or build a fence."

The two women marched down the hill, their high heels snapping against the gravel of the driveway. Mary looked back just before sliding into her Volvo.

"You can forget that swimming invitation," Nadean shouted. Her knees buckled; she grabbed Woodrow's arm to keep from falling. A breeze crested the hill, stirring the fine, white sand, sweeping skyward a few grains of Paradise.

Over the following days, the residents of Oak Hills became more and more divided over Woodrow's yard. Nadean, following her initial rage, was embarrassed and saddened that her beach was causing such problems. She had assumed others would find it as beautiful as she did, had intended for the beach to become a gathering place on summer afternoons for the neighbors. She was especially saddened that Mary led the charges.

Why they so up tight, Nadean wondered, over nothing but a pretty spot, a little color. Think everyone's yard got to look the same? That ole clipped grass, carved-up bushes, tar driveways— ain't no wildness in it. Let a mushroom dare poke his head up, and they chop him right off. Nobody can't give the dandelion time to open his puffball 'fore they get out the hoe. One of them plant a maple tree, everybody on the street go tearing out to get one. Ain't no wildness in these people.

But who am I? No better. What'd I do, go running off think- ing weren't nothing worse than a tobacco field. First thing, crammed my ass in the tightest skirt I could find, just like all the other ladies. Got my hair ironed. Drank Schlitz Bull. Who am I now? Like that boy in the Bible who comes crawling home 'specting to still get what he ain't helped earn.

Nadean took Woodrow's hand and led him to the front porch. "This here your land, Woodrow. Was your daddy's land. You always live a life of peace, then I come along and stir things up. You want to cut that palm down, go ahead. There won't be no fuss from me." She held her breath.

Woodrow walked down the steps to the center of the front yard, then turned in a slow circle. Evening was settling and the air was cooling rapidly. He moved his mouth as if tasting the twi- light. One of the hounds yelped at a silver moon rising over the treetops.

Woodrow hunting, the chase carrying the length of the ridge. Mary sleepless, listening. Angry.

That man acts as if he owns this community, she thought.

Thinks just because his family has been here so long, he has the right to trample over other people.

The image of the palm was stamped on her retina. She tried to blink it away, but each time it returned, slowly, like a photograph drawing to focus in a pan of solution.

The community council had met again and decided to attend the next meeting of the county commissioners. There, they would request that a building code be enacted that would govern Oak Hills.

The sounds of the hunt maddened Mary. The baying of the hounds mixed and lapped with blasts from the horn, ebbed, rose, and returned in slow cycles. The act illustrated Woodrow's lunacy, Mary decided. A man hunting alone at night, chasing a pack of dogs over hill and valley, through creeks and ravines. Blowing on a damn horn like a child playing with a kazoo. Is that the explanation? Is Bunce a child? That blank look of his, shy smile, and few words. Is he forever locked in childhood?

Mary had researched and studied Woodrow's history, his return from Vietnam, his naked escapade in the chinaberry tree. Now she feared he had a dangerous side, imagined Woodrow running, his clothes torn away, feet scratched and bloody, eyes bright with craze, pausing to lift his horn and call to whatever demon he followed. She snuggled closer to Jeffery.

Jeffery hoped so bad they were already pregnant. Just that night he had said it again.

"Let's have him now, honey, while we are young and can enjoy him," Jeffery reasoned.

Mary stroked Jeffery's shoulder. A baby? What in the world would she do with a baby? Sometimes she still felt like a baby herself. And now the job to complicate her life. Of all times.

Mary had gone Tuesday for an interview at the journalism school. She knew she did well. The dean told her a decision would be made in a week. She still hadn't mentioned the job to Jeffery.

Oh damn! In many ways, he's right. We should get pregnant. We're healthy. We have the money. Our marriage is fine. Most of our friends are having kids. If I made a list, it would be lopsided in favor of having children. But, what would it do to me ever having a career?

Mary recalled another day from her hitchhiking that had stuck in her memory—Iowa, flat fields to the horizon, a squat, wooden house not thirty feet from the narrow blacktop road. As she came up beside the house, she watched a woman hanging her wash on a rusty clothesline—some on the branches of a bush—men's shirts, heavy work trousers, child's polo shirts, tiny dresses, stained cloth diapers. The clothes were heavy with water and hung straight down in the wind. A baby sat on a blanket behind the woman. She cried, her wail unheeded by her mother. An older boy tossed rocks at an empty beer can. The can skittered across the gravelly soil. A man's voice boomed through the open front door. "Yeah," the woman shouted.

A hound spied Mary, began barking. The woman turned, stared, then hushed the dog. Mary hunched her shoulders, jerking her heavy pack higher. She kept walking. The boy stopped tossing rocks and walked to the shoulder of the road, staring dumbly. The mother examined Mary's pack, the faded jeans she wore, the oak staff she held that thudded against the ground with every other step. The woman stared with wide, shiny eyes.

The boy had the sniffles. He sucked back a trail of snot. The baby screamed to be held. Mary nodded quickly to the woman. The woman slowly lifted one hand, her fingers spread and stiff. The man shouted again, and she dropped her hand.

Mary passed behind a hedge, leaving the mother, her rickety house, and wind-chapped children. Mary heard a rock skip across the pavement behind her.

She had carried that image since—the mother's hand held in

timid salute, fingers red and peeling from wash water, her hair pulled back in a bun that spilled limp strands. The woman represented everything that Mary feared.

Jeffery stirred. Mary caressed the fine hairs that grew on the small of his neck. "Love you, babe," she whispered. "My husband, lover, my best friend. I'm so lucky."

After the Rockies, everything in her upper-middle-class life seemed either tragic or silly, an existence filled with trivia and formality. All she wanted then was a small house beside the forest where she could smell fresh air, grow vegetables minus poisonous chemicals, and feel free to sit with her feet up and smoke a joint on summer evenings. And all her mother wanted was for her and Jeffery to marry and begin the life they were bred and educated for—him to provide the livelihood, and her to raise children and be a good homemaker and spouse. Jeffery was of the same school.

The wedding had been a nightmare. Mary wanted a simple ceremony outdoors with a few friends and family members attending. Her mother cried for a church wedding that was at least equal to any of her peers. She endured two bridal showers, a rehearsal dinner, white-tie wedding, and a reception with an open bar and orchestra. She and her mother gulped ten-milligram Valiums.

Mary remembered how tough that first year of marriage had proven. Jeffery's job forced a move upstate. He worked long hours and traveled weekly. Mary found she was overly educated for the local job market. Getting used to the daily habits of another person proved harder than she had imagined. For several months, if they were not arguing, they were making love, and making love was like fighting. Without the strength of wedding vows, Mary feared one of them might have walked out.

But slowly, life had smoothed out. They both just needed time to rid themselves of silly illusions. There were rules and standards expected of adults, and sooner or later, the mature played the game. Wildness, you outgrew if you were smart.

Mary had to prove that to Woodrow. You have to play team ball sooner or later. Two breakdowns had to be suffered before she realized that blue jeans, pot, and an open road weren't the answers to life's problems.

But God! A baby? Mary Stewert the mother of a baby? In the same league as the woman in Iowa. Mary the aspiring journalism professor settling for a life as Mary the diaper washer? Wasn't it just possible that her mother and Jeffery were mistaken—that the two could be combined?

Woodrow's hounds crested the ridge. Their baying was smothered as the hounds dropped into the thick forest that bordered Haw River. Mary heard a lone, thin note from Woodrow's horn. She rolled and clung to her husband's back, covering her head with the blanket.

Benson Bunce stood before his dark bedroom window, staring at his reflection in the glass. His breath slowly clouded the pane.

God damn Woodrow, he thought. Damn boy is crazier than I ever thought. He gonna end up causing more trouble in this community than people have seen in fifty years.

He pressed his forehead to the cold pane, looking beyond his reflection. On the dark curve of a far hill, he glimpsed a flicker of light. Must be Woodrow's lantern? The light did not reappear. Probably imagined it.

Benson was irritated to find himself again fingering the small knot on his testicle. He snatched his hand away.

He had discovered the knot several days ago while bathing, ignored it under the sun, but worried at night. Probably just a cyst, he thought. Probably go away if I'd leave it alone. The knot was hardly big as a pea.

Again, Benson glimpsed the flicker of light. "You better keep running, little brother," he whispered, "on over the crest of that hill and toward the Blue Ridge, 'cause I fear they're closing in on you."

Two days ago, a group from the subdivision had visited Benson. They asked that he persuade Woodrow to clean up his yard. Benson didn't blame them for being upset. Woodrow's beach was just about the gaudiest thing he had ever seen, but still, he couldn't help defending his brother. Woodrow was flesh, crazy or not, and besides, a man had a right to build what he pleased on his land.

Margo rolled onto her back, then sat up in bed. She felt for Benson, then called his name.

"I'm right here, honey."

"What are you doing up? Come back to bed."

"Will in just a second," he answered. "I'm getting some water." In seconds, she slept again.

Benson was always amazed that she could detect his absence even from her sleep. In twenty-two years of marriage, they had only been apart for two nights, and that was when the children were born. He knew her so damn well, every shade of her personality, every wrinkle, soft crease, and mole. Maybe he knew her too well? Ain't no mystery no more, just two cogs in a machine, turning against each other.

Without understanding exactly why, he had driven by Reba's old place the day before. He hadn't stopped, only slowed at the long drive leading to her house. Even with the distance, he saw that the paint was peeling, the yard grown over. The ruts he had helped wear in the clay road were washed smooth.

Benson swore softly when he found his hand fingering the knot. He held the windowsill with both hands, tried to recall the shape of Reba's face. All those years of sharing her covers, and now he found it hard to remember exactly the slope of her nose, how her breasts swung when she walked. Wasn't that hourglass birthmark on her left thigh?

Remember how she always stood in the doorway to the bedroom before switching off the light. What a figure, those high hipbones and long legs. Looked like she needed a couple extra spoonfuls at supper. But only a couple. She'd prance across the room and slip under the covers, roll up against me, smell like soap and toothpaste. Damn, we made that bed rock. Then we'd lay there for maybe half an hour, talking silly to each other, rubbing each other, sometimes even do it again. I'd slap that high rump of hers when she got up, then lay there half asleep while she brought me a water glass half filled with whiskey.

Margo mumbled something in her sleep. Benson's mind returned from Reba. Got me a fine wife over there. Why I want to think the way I am? She loves me, ain't refused me once, birthed my children, raised them. Tomorrow morning, she'll be out of bed before me, cooking sausage and biscuits and brewing coffee. And here I am, panting over a damn half-breed.

Benson heard a far peal from Woodrow's horn. In the window reflection, he saw himself in a doctor's office, sitting on the edge of a chair. The doctor studied a medical report, his lips pulled tight over his teeth.

"I'm sorry, Mr. Bunce. It's bad news." He lowered the report. "I'm afraid it's malignant."

Benson swallowed, held tight to the chair arms. He nodded. "Which means what?" he forced out.

The doctor looked him straight in his eyes. "Surgery, I'm afraid. Maybe we can save one testicle."

Benson closed his eyes to erase the vision. He deliberately felt the knot. Ain't grown none in a week, he decided. Thing ain't big as my little fingernail. Just a cyst. It'd probably go away if I'd leave it alone.

Benson spied the light one final time. It shone for several seconds from a clearing on the hillside. He lamented that the family had once owned that entire ridge, owned most of the land he could see if he was outside and turned in a circle. Most of it was sold off now, snapped up by developers. Benson reckoned the coming summer would be his last at farming tobacco. Tobacco just wasn't worth the trouble. Not without Woodrow to help out. Not with the wages people demanded now, and those damn social workers always inquiring about the migrant help. What the hell, anyway—he was set financially for life. The second boy was finishing college this year. The only damn thing in the world worrying him was Woodrow—and the lump.

Ahhh, lump ain't shit. That God damn Woodrow, I don't know what to do about. I can't fault him just for planting a palm tree. Can't fault a man for doing what's in his heart.

A trickle of condensation on the pane. Benson saw a river, down south in the bayou country Reba had told him stories— sugarcane growing right up to the water, alligators, oranges you could pick in your backyard. He saw Reba wearing a cotton dress, the silhouette of her legs showing as she walked barefoot across a plowed field to bring him cold tea.

Shit. I could just take off, leave Margo with enough to live good the rest of her life, and still have plenty to buy some little fifty-acre farm. Land that ain't spoiled and crowded. Reba, she could make a comfortable home out of a hog parlor.

Margo called in her sleep. Benson wiped the river away with one fingertip. Get that slut out of your mind, man. You're thinking as damn crazy as Woodrow.

Benson opened the window a couple of inches. The cold air felt good on his face. He listened for the hunt, but heard only a car pass.

"You better run, Woodrow," he whispered. " 'Cause whatever you chase out there, it's leaving Oak Hills. God knows, it's already left me."

Under a large moon, Woodrow sucked cold air deep into his lungs, then blew out hot breath from deep in his lungs. The vapor fanned to a white cloud. His heavy boot tread was worn nearly smooth from years of grinding against granite and feldspar, his wind coming in gasps as his boots grabbed the hillside, slid back a half step, grabbed, his weight carried on the balls of his feet.

The hounds bayed like demons, their noses gorged with blood as they followed the scent of wildlife downhill toward the river land.

Woodrow heard his own heart pounding in the well of his ears; head down, he crashed through a final bramble of wilted honeysuckle vines and onto a bald hilltop, cocked his head, and listened—the dogs have treed—their baying gone from the short yelps of chase to sorrowful long cries.

Woodrow placed his forefinger against his nostril, bent slightly, and blew a wad of snot that carried in a sideward arc of several feet, then cleared the other sinus. Breathing easier, he lifted the horn from its sling of rawhide. Fitting his lips to the mouthpiece, he tucked the small of his tongue into the groove and blew. A short, powerful blast rolled through the nude branches and climbed skyward. Another blast. The hounds answered in unison, guiding him with bass tones.

Scrambling downhill, Woodrow braked with his heels, tree trunks starkly white in the beam of his lantern, they thinned from oaks to sweet gum and pine. A covey of sleeping quail were flushed, frantic wings beating louder than his heart. The dogs bayed long and sad, he lifted his horn again and rent the air with short trumpets.

The air smelled of water. The hounds ringed a cypress tree, the bitches baying from their haunches, the young male yelping with his forefeet against the trunk. They ignored Woodrow's light, intent on the musk of raccoon thirty feet above.

Woodrow directed his lantern beam, followed the trunk upward—limbs bare of foliage, he spied the raccoon huddled close to the trunk. She stared into the blinding light, then slowly turned her head and hunkered tight against her poor shelter.

Woodrow stared for a moment, then raised his horn and blew a single long blast that filled every space between atoms.

The hounds reluctantly turned from the tree, put their noses to the ground, and began running in widening circles. Yards into the woods, the oldest bitch sniffed the trail of rabbit, yelped, her son answered. Woodrow turned from the cypress with a single long stride. He raised his horn and called pursuit. He climbed again toward the feldspar and granite chips that littered the porous soil where oaks grew.

Woodrow crashed through the bramble, barely outdistanced by the arc of his light, his balance held in check between his head-down lunge and the resistance of the forest. The hounds bayed the direction of their hunt. Woodrow lifted his horn to answer, that instant stumbling and falling. He flung out his arms to break the fall.

Woodrow landed heavily on his belly, his lantern skittered ahead of him across the ground. He crawled to it, wiped dirt from the lens, then shone the beam in a circle. A six-foot-wide path had been cleared across the ridge. Woodrow stared at the red flags of a survey crew, at trees upheaved by a bulldozer blade. The air was pungent with turned soil. Woodrow shone his beam up and down the furrow, saw it disappear as it dropped to both sides of the hill. The furrow resembled a gash. Woodrow turned over his palm and saw it had been cut by a splinter of wood.

Woodrow lifted his horn again, but this time bellowed pain and sorrow into the mouthpiece. The cry rolled over the ridge top and down the slope toward town, swallowing all the night sounds.

Nadean read the luminous dial on the alarm clock. Two in the morning. She had listened to the hounds run the length of the ridge, their baying now muted by the forest.

Tonight, more than ever, the sounds of the hunt bothered her. As Nadean listened, she was struck with a flash of memory, as if she had heard the hounds and horn from some earlier time and place far from Oak Hills. But that was silly.

What do I care? A grown man got to have his reasons for running through the dark woods. If it don't scare him, why I let it bother me?

As she stared into the dark of the ceiling, a thought came to her that made her pull the covers over her chin. She imagined the hounds actually chasing Woodrow, him running, stumbling, blowing his horn so someone might come to his aid.

Silly woman, she told herself. You better stop watching that ole "Twilight Zone."

But they chasing something out there. Dog don't bark like that 'less he after something. Maybe there some poor possum or coon running for his life?

In the last couple of weeks, Nadean had begun to feel hunted. At times she felt like skinning up the palm tree to the high fronds where she could no longer hear the complaints of her neighbors.

How they ever get so upset over a tree, Lord, I can't understand. These same folks that made a fuss over me, while people in town calling me nigger. The same folks that were all worried over the eagles. What can they see wrong in a palm tree? That tree is new and pure like I am now. Like Jerome said I couldn't ever be.

Nadean huddled over a nasty toilet minus the seat. Jerome bumped her with the toe of his shoe.

"You ain't tended your corner in two nights. What da fuck you think this is, vacation?"

Nadean rolled from his foot, away from the stench of her vomit. Her tears split Jerome's face into brown splinters.

"Baby, I'm sick," she cried. "Can't you see? I'm sick. I need help."

"Shit. Only help you want is another needle. You wouldn't see no doctor if I carried you to his front door."

Jerome sat on the edge of the bare, single bed, the springs squealing. He leaned forward, his hands on his knees. "This needle is gonna quit coming, too, if you don't get on back to work. How long it take you to learn? You ain't on the farm. Don't shit come free in the city."

Nadean tried to vomit again, but her stomach was dry. She staggered to the sink and drank from the faucet. After several gulps, she retched.

"Lord, gal, you ought to see yourself," Jerome said. "Your folks wouldn't know you right now."

Nadean turned, still holding to the sink. A dribble of saliva hung on her lip. "Why you doing this to me?" she cried. "You told me I was pretty. Talked how pretty I could sing. Why, Jerome?"

Jerome chuckled meanly. "Girl, you still dumb as the day you trotted 'way from that baccor field." He narrowed his eyes. "Don't you understand the game yet? Every bitch ever worked for me, I told her she was pretty. Had half of them thinking they could sing worth a damn. I knew sooner or later where they'd be."

Nadean closed her eyes and slumped against the wall. She wished she held a gun so she could kill him, then herself. Suddenly she lurched at Jerome. He shoved her to the floor where she lay sobbing.

After a couple of minutes, Jerome walked across the room and kneeled beside Nadean. He touched her matted hair, her cheek. "Babe," he began softly, "you were pretty. Damn prettiest thing I ever saw that day you were standing by the street. No makeup. That plain dress. Looking at you was like going home." He lifted her chin. "I'm gonna do something I ain't before. Maybe I'm getting soft."

Jerome counted four twenties from his wallet. He stuffed the money in Nadean's blouse. "I'm through with ya. You can take this money and run it up your arm, or you can get a bus back home. I'd like to think you'll go home, but I doubt it. There just some people born to be a whore. They weak. I don't know. Hate themselves, maybe. They don't love nothing. They pushed around their whole life."

He began tying a shoelace tightly around her forearm. "Songbird. That's the way the animal kingdom works. There's the weak. And there's the strong."

Nadean rose from her bed and walked to the window. No longer did she hear the hounds.

"No, Jerome," she whispered. "You were right 'bout some things, but not all of them. A body can change. I got my feet back in the ground, and I'm getting strong. Starting to love some things. Growing tall as that palm tree."

From down the hallway, Nadean heard the creak of Ellis's bedsprings. He coughed.

I been running away all my life, but I'm home now, she thought. Nadean ain't gonna be pushed around no more.

Ellis was drawn from sleep by the creak of his bedroom door. He heard soft footsteps walk up to the edge of his bed.

"Ellis, honey, you awake?" he heard Nadean whisper.

"Yeah, ah, sure," he said. He propped on one elbow. "Something the matter?"

"No." She shook her head, balling the fingers of one hand and releasing them repeatedly. After several seconds had passed, she sat on the edge of his bed. "No, nothing's the matter. Guess I'm kind of lonely, that's all. Sometimes them hounds running scare me. I don't know why. They ever scare you?"

"Naw. Used to when I was a kid. Made me have bad dreams. Now, I don't pay them much attention."

"They don't usually bother me so much," Nadean said. "Just tonight. Guess I'm worrying too much 'bout the fuss people are making over the beach."

"Awww, piss on the whole crowd," Ellis answered. "They'll get over it sooner or later."

Nadean patted Ellis's knee. "You make me feel better. Say, why you awake if you ain't scared?"

"Oh, I was dozing some. I got a test tomorrow I didn't study too well for."

Ellis was bothered that Nadean rested her hand on his knee. Slowly she kneaded his skin. Ellis's eyes were becoming accustomed to the darkness. He studied Nadean's silhouette. She wore only her slip, the thin shoulder straps luminous against her dark skin, a darker triangle of shadow above her breasts. Suddenly, she hunched her shoulders and shivered.

"You cold?" Ellis asked.

"No. Rabbit just run 'cross my grave," she answered. Nadean hugged her arms to her bosom. The crease of light through the doorway cast a halo about her hair. She rocked slowly.

"Maybe the heat needs to be turned up some?" Ellis said.

"No, honey, it just them dogs running. Like they chasing something and it running and running. You ever think about how it would feel to be chased?"

Ellis pushed off the mattress until his back was against the headboard. "Want me to get up and us talk for a while? I could make you some chocolate or something."

Nadean shook her head. Her hands fluttered about in her lap like a fallen bird. "Ellis, you and Woodrow my family now. Like my own blood. I love my family."

Ellis swallowed loudly and nodded.

"Do you love this place, Ellis? Is it home to you?"

"It's the closest thing I've ever felt to home," Ellis answered. "More than that damn place I come from."

"We may have to fight, Ellis. Them people serious. I don't think Woodrow knows how serious they are."

"Oh, they're serious, all right," Ellis answered. "Woodrow wouldn't worry if a nuclear war started."

"We gonna have to stick together, Ellis," Nadean said. "Me and you in the same boat, got a good thing for the first time in our lives. You gonna fight, Ellis?"

"Damn right," he answered. "I'm ready to kick Jeffery Stewert's ass right now." He looked out the window at the few lights shining in the community. "We have the high ground, Nadean. That's where you want to fight from, on the top of the hill."

"That's right," Nadean answered, a slow smile creasing her face. "We have the high ground. We living closest to heaven." Nadean stood. "You go to sleep, Ellis. I'm feeling better now. Them people have to look up to us 'cause we have the high ground."

Ellis watched Nadean walk back to her room, her dark figure disappearing in shadows. A thought came to him then, one of the few facts he had retained for his history test—a bugle sounding as Custer and his men retreated for the hilltop above the Little Bighorn.

14

The county commissioners met on their regular second Monday of the month. Mary and several members of the community council sat in the front row of benches. When Mary's name was finally called, she took two deep breaths, then walked to the podium holding a handful of papers.

"Commissioners," chairman Harry Clark began, "we've received a request from a coalition of citizens from the Oak Hills community, asking that we consider their request for a community building code." He nodded sharply at Mary. "What can we help you with, Mrs. Stewert?"

Mary returned his greeting, swallowed, then took another breath. "I thank you, commissioners, for hearing us tonight." She shuffled her papers, waiting for her pulse to slow. Following another breath, she began. "Commissioners, I'm sure that all of you are aware of the rapid growth in Oak Hills. In the past two years alone, the population has doubled after having stayed stationary for the past fifty years. A study has shown that with the coming completion of Interstate 40, our population could again double in three to four years. There is a nearly unanimous feeling among the residents of Oak Hills that guidelines must be established that will help control this explosive growth and ensure that the quality of life we enjoy now is preserved."

Mary paused, her eyes sweeping the five men who made up the commission. Breathe again, she told herself. Relax. They're normal humans just like yourself.

Clark nodded, removed his glasses, and began wiping them with a handkerchief. "Well, I'm not that familiar with Oak Hills, Mrs. Stewert, since I live north of Chapel Hill, but I do know this entire area is growing like a brush fire." Clark held his glasses to the ceiling lights, inspected the clear lenses, then placed them upon his nose. "Have the members of the coalition decided upon what type of building code you would like to see enforced?"

Mary slipped a second page from the bottom of the stack of papers. Breathe again. Keep your voice strong, head up. "Yes, Mr. Chairman. We've discussed the matter at length, even studied the policies of some other communities. We've decided on several requirements."

"All right. Why don't you read them to us."

Mary tilted the page. "First, we would like a requirement that all future homes built in Oak Hills be valued at a minimum of seventy thousand dollars. This would ensure that the property of those people who pioneered this community is not devalued. Second, we would like a ruling passed that all additions to property not linked directly to the main residence—such as patios, pools, workshops—be screened from public view by fences or shrubbery. Third, we would like a measure passed that bans any construction or placement of objects not connected to the main residence that exceed ten feet in height. We would also like these three measures, if enacted, to become retroactive to the first of this year."

Mary stared in turn into each commissioner's face. Clark scribbled on a sheet of paper. Mary glanced back at Jeffery, who gave her a thumbs-up.

Clark sat back in his chair. "Well, Mrs. Stewert, it's obvious that you've come well prepared tonight. The way we usually try to handle community building codes is to let the citizens have what they want, as long as the request doesn't interfere with local laws and has majority consent. The next step would be for us to vote for a public hearing at a future meeting to listen to what pros or cons might arise, then, for us to vote on the code. Do you understand?"

"Yes, Mr. Chairman," Mary answered. "I understand that, and ask please that a hearing be scheduled as soon as possible."

Clark looked at the other commissioners on his left and right. "Is there any discussion before a motion is called to schedule a public hearing?"

Commissioner Canady, a rawboned, lanky man with tousled brown hair, lifted his hand. He leaned over his desk, his hands clasped. "Mrs. Stewert," he began slowly. "I grew up in Oak Hills, so I'm very aware of the rapid growth you spoke of. When I was living there, maybe five families made up the entire place: the Garners, the Tuckers, the Bunces—a few others. You said this building code is to protect the property of the people who pioneered Oak Hills. How long have you been living in the community?"

Mary's face suddenly burned, and her throat scratched when she tried to swallow. "Mr. Canady, my husband and I have lived in Oak Hills for more than a year."

"I see. In the subdivision?"

Mary's heart began racing again, her balloon of confidence flagging. "Yes. The Whispering Pines subdivision."

Canady stared at his desk. He separated his hands and drummed his fingers against the wood for a moment. "Is there any particular circumstance that has prompted your coalition to request a building code?"

Mary stared darkly at Canady. Might know there would be one troublemaker in the group, she thought. She cleared her throat. "A concern for our community is our primary motivation," Mary answered.

Canady nodded. "So, Woodrow Bunce's place has nothing to do with this?"

Mary felt her tongue swelling. She opened her mouth, but no words came out.

"Who is Woodrow Bunce?" Clark asked.

Canady turned to the chairman. "Bunce is a local farmer who has stirred up controversy lately by transplanting a palm tree in his front yard."

Mary's anger forced her tongue to move. "Mr. Chairman, we are concerned with the entire community of Oak Hills, and are not acting over one individual. I promise you."

Mark Serles, a commissioner sitting at the opposite end of the bench from Canady, spoke up. "Mr. Chairman. I'm familiar with the controversy in Oak Hills. Bunce's new pool and palm tree have been nicknamed 'the beach.' Frankly, I don't feel I'm being out of line by saying it's caused quite a stir."

Mary nodded at Serles. She felt a tide of confidence returning.

Clark shook his head. "Only in this county." He tapped his desk with his pencil eraser. "Do I have a motion that a public hearing be scheduled for the next regular meeting of the county commissioners concerning a building code for the Oak Hills community?"

"So moved," Serles answered.

"Do I have a second?"

"Second," said commissioner Ben Hair.

"There is a motion and a second that a public hearing be set for the next meeting to hear arguments concerning a building code in Oak Hills. Those in favor raise your right arms."

The motion passed unanimously. Mary and her entourage left the meeting and shared a couple bottles of champagne.

Tongue and telephone spread the news of the public hearing. Mary set up a command post in her study. The general store in Oak Hills became the gathering place for those opposed to a building code.

Midweek, thirty people crowded into the store following supper at the request of commissioner James Canady. Canady had spent his youth in Oak Hills before leaving to join the navy. He now owned and operated a large hardware store in Carrboro, his widowed aunt the only relative left in the community.

People perched on top of upturned soda crates, on the edge of the wooden counter, the oldest women getting the few cane-backed chairs. A cat dozed under the edge of the oil heater, safe from the teeth of a curious beagle. After the greetings and small talk wound down, Canady stepped to the front of the crowd.

"Folks, I realize that as an elected official, it's my duty to represent the majority interests of Oak Hills. But, ya'll know, too, I grew up here, and it's impossible for me not to have strong feelings for this community. I just want to talk with everyone tonight and explain what it will mean if a building code is passed next week."

Canady turned to Woodrow, who towered at the rear of the crowd. "Woodrow, I reckon you know the main reason the subdivision people are after a building code is because of your front yard?"

"Yeah. Seems to be."

"Okay. I just wanted to be right up front," Canady said. "Woodrow, you have to admit, your yard doesn't exactly blend with the surrounding property."

"The Bunces owned that land years before anyone thought twice about a subdivision," Buck Melvin said.

"That's right," Bob Garner answered. "It's getting around here where if you drive a pickup truck, people look at you funny."

Canady lifted his hand. "I agree. What you're saying is all true, but the fact is, this county is changing. It's growing and is going to keep on growing. Ten years from now, I'd venture to say that not five people will be left in Oak Hills that lived here during World War Two."

The store door opened and several more people entered. In the group was Benson Bunce. Benson took a place in the crowd on the opposite side of the room from his brother. Woodrow nodded at him. Benson looked away.

"What the hell is a building code, anyway?" someone asked.

"A building code regulates what you can do with your land," Canady explained. "It's what the majority says they want visible from the road or from the air or maybe just from their front windows. Most of the people in the subdivision don't like the looks of Woodrow's palm tree and beach. They think it's ugly."

"You ask me, ugly is all those houses built where we used to have woods and fields," Bob Garner said.

"What about those damn ugly satellite dishes everyone in there has pointed at the moon?"

Canady raised his hand again. "Maybe to you, that's ugly. Maybe to me, too. But the point I'm trying to make is you and me ain't the majority any longer in Oak Hills. It doesn't matter if someone has lived here only a week, he has an equal voice in how he wants the community to look."

Horace Tucker, an old black man wearing bib overalls, his jaw big with a wad of tobacco, stood up. "Mr. Canady, I got a chicken coop that is visible from the road. Had it for probably thirty years. You saying that if people say it's ugly, I got to tear it down?"

"That could happen, Horace. If enough people wanted it that way."

Miss Penny stood up, her apron still tied around her stout waist. "Jimmy, I been growing collards each winter down the side of my yard since I can remember. What if folks get to thinking collard plants are ugly?"

"If they list it under the building code, the collards would have to go."

A murmur rolled through the crowd. Woodrow fidgeted, fingering a button on his shirt. He shifted his weight from foot to foot. When he began speaking, his slow words were like a growl against the quick arguments.

"Folks, ah, well, ah. I never meant to cause this trouble." He licked his lips noisily. Nadean put her hand on his arm. "That tree, well, ah, I figured people would like it the same as we do." Woodrow furrowed his hair with his fingers. "But it ain't worth causing trouble. I can cut it down tomorrow. No, I'll do it tonight."

Everyone was quiet for several seconds, surprised by the longest speech they had ever heard from Woodrow. Nadean's eyes grew wide with dread. Finally, Canady broke the silence.

"I don't think it's just the palm tree, Woodrow. I think the building code is the accumulation of a whole lot of things."

"Don't touch that tree, son," Tucker said. "It's a sad time a man can't do what he want on land that his family own for years and years."

"Horace is right," Miss Penny said. "You cut down that tree, next week they'll be telling me to snatch up my collards. The week after that, they're liable to tell me to move my little snack bar right on out of town. You leave that tree where it stands."

A chorus of "keep that tree," a few "hell, yeah"s rose from the crowd. The shouting woke the cat, who cast a baleful yellow eye on the beagle.

From the back of the room, Mack Lupo spoke up. He stood beside his two brothers, Bill and Wayne. "I heard there's talk of developing Thunder Ridge. Is that right?"

All eyes in the room turned to Mack. Many of the people in the room had been at Woodrow's last party and remembered the trouble. Mack stared back at the people, many averting their eyes.

"There's talk of it," Canady answered. "It's being surveyed now."

Mack turned to Benson Bunce. "Ain't you rich enough, Benson? You've done sold half this town away to strangers. Can't you leave the ridge? I've hunted it since I was little." He pointed at Woodrow. "Your brother hunts it."

Benson took a deep breath, his face coloring with anger. "I don't own that damn ridge. Consolidated Paper has owned it since the depression. What they do, I have no control over."

"Well, if you hadn't sold land right up to it, they wouldn't even think of developing it."

"You listen here, son," Benson said, "what I do ain't none—"

Canady held up his hand and interrupted the argument. "Let's don't get to arguing among ourselves," he said. "That's the last thing we need. The way realty has increased in value around here, it was just a matter of time before that timberland was sold. What we want to do is try and keep the community right here untouched."

A round of small arguments began, different people blaming different causes for the development.

"I have to be honest with ya'll," Canady said after the din had subsided. "I imagine this building code will be passed, majority rules the land. But, if enough of you turn out for this hearing, there's a chance. A small chance."

The cat stretched his back. The small dog growled. A Mountain Dew bottle was opened, signaling the end of the meeting.

Following the meeting, the Lupo brothers gathered in a knot at the tailgate of Mack's truck. Mack lit a cigarette, his hand still trembling with anger. "They start tearing into that ridge, we're fucked. Ya'll know that."

Wayne Lupo, three years younger than Mack, spoke up. "Well, maybe it's a sign, Mack. Maybe it's a sign that we ought to quit this business before we get busted."

"I agree," Bill said. "Mack, I'm tired of looking over my shoulder all the time. The way they use them airplanes now, next year we might get caught. I don't want to spend ten years in jail."

Mack blew out smoke. "It ain't our land. They can't trace it to us. We're all twenty thousand dollars richer today because of that dope crop. We got to do it at least one more year."

"There's other jobs, Mack. Why chance it another year?"

"There ain't other jobs for me. Farming ain't shit no more. Ya'll two know heating and air conditioning 'cause you were at the technical school while I was layin' in the mud in Nam." Mack sucked at his cigarette again. "I got to go at it one more year and I need your help. One last big crop." He kicked at a root exposed on the ground. "Just this morning, Nancy told me she's pregnant again."

Bingo. Mary was pregnant. She knew the answer even before the doctor told her the test results. Jeffery was too thorough in everything he undertook to have failed. Jeffery believed in perfection.

"Are you pleased?" the doctor asked.

Mary smiled. "Of course. I'm delighted." Above the doctor's

head floated a dim image of the Iowa washerwoman. Her chapped hand was raised in salute.

"Welcome to the club," the woman whispered.

Mary stopped halfway across the parking lot and held to a light pole while a bout of dizziness passed.

Morning sickness already? He said I was only seven weeks. Must just be the excitement. Oh God, please don't let me throw up in front of everyone.

Mary closed her eyes and gulped air. Once inside her car, she rested with her seat leaned back.

I can't believe it. Mary Stewert pregnant. Jeffery will just die. Mary rested until she had passed the danger of throwing up, then drove to a pay phone and dialed Jeffery's office. She liked his manner of answering—powerful and urgent—as if he were granting a person a favor by allowing them his time.

"Hello, Papa," she said.

Silence. "What did you just say?"

"I said, *Hello, Papa.*"

Mr. Powerful's voice trembled while he told her of his love.

During the drive home, Mary stopped twice to let bouts of nausea pass. She couldn't help smiling, remembering Jeffery's plea that she be especially careful driving. She was surprised to find his car already in the driveway when she arrived. He met her halfway across the lawn, hugged her gently, then lifted her and carried her into the house.

"From today on, it's rest time for you, understand?" Jeffery said. "I'll hire someone to come in and help with the housework."

"Oh, don't be silly. I'm only pregnant. It's not like I have a disease or a broken bone." She loved the attention.

For lunch, he cooked her a T-bone steak. They toasted the pregnancy with Perrier and a twist. Alcohol was banned from both their diets for the next seven months.

"Let's see," Jeffery figured. "Columbia. Class of 2006, isn't it? Sure to become a senator if he has half his mother's spunk."

Twice, Mary's lunch was interrupted by calls from members of the coalition.

"It's cut-and-dry," William Bates, a lawyer, said. "I've already talked with two members of the commission, and they've assured me the hearing is all formality. Bunce will be cleaning up his act inside of a month."

Mary had barely sat down when June Kent called. "Mary, I have at least a hundred people who have sworn to attend the hearing." She squealed when Mary told her about the baby. "That's wonderful, Mary. And it's about time. I was beginning to wonder if you and Jeffery ever got together with all the work you're doing."

"Oh, we got together all right," Mary said and laughed. "And Bill just called and said that as soon as the code is voted in, Bunce will have about a month to comply."

"Well, I hope so," June answered. "My parents are coming to visit in July, and Mother would just die if she saw that yard. Oh, Mary! I'm so excited about the baby."

Jeffery swore when the phone rang a third time. "I'll be glad when this building code business is all over."

Oh, June, Mary thought as she lifted the receiver. I bet she's called a dozen people to tell them about the baby. "Hello."

"Yes. Hello," an unfamiliar male voice responded. "Is this the residence of Mary Stewert?"

"You're speaking with her."

"Hello, Mary. My name is Charlie Gains, the dean of the journalism school at UNC. I'd like to talk with you about coming to work for us."

The phone slipped from Mary's hand, bouncing twice on the carpet. The line was dead when she put it back to her ear. "Hello," Mary shouted above the dial tone.

The wall clock suddenly chimed. The wooden bird leaped from his nest. "Cuckoo," he quipped. "Cuckoo."

15

he press was tipped of the battle brewing in Oak Hills. A camera crew was sent from a local television station to film the story. Ellis answered a knock on the door to face an attractive young woman.

"Hello. You must be Ellis," she said. "I'm Donna Pawley from Action News in Raleigh. We've heard of the plight you're in over your yard, and would like to do a story."

Ellis gulped, staring at his reflection in a camera lens. He tugged at his collar while shouting for Woodrow. Woodrow came to the door, drying dishwater from his hands with a wash-cloth. The camera lens glinted sunlight.

Donna stepped forward, thrusting out her hand. "Mr. Bunce, I'm Donna Pawley with Action News, and we're very concerned over the problem you're having with some of your neighbors. We would like to do a story for tonight's news."

Woodrow wadded the towel, then tossed it inside the door. He called Nadean. Donna repeated her story.

"Do a story 'bout us?" Nadean said. "How did ya'll hear 'bout this mess?" She pushed at a sprig of hair that dangled over one eye.

"Someone called the station. Your situation is the type of human-interest story we look for."

Nadean hunched one shoulder, moving a half step behind Woodrow. She wished she had washed her hair. Woodrow stared over Donna's head.

"Come on, let's do it," Ellis said, tugging at Nadean's arm. "I've never been on television."

Woodrow, Nadean, and Ellis stood shoulder to shoulder upon the beach, the palm tree swaying behind. The crew moved two of the flamingos so that they showed on camera. Donna touched up her makeup. Nadean wished she had a brush.

"Rolling," a man shouted. The camera clicked.

"This is Donna Pawley for Action News, and today we are visiting the home of Woodrow Bunce in the picturesque community of Oak Hills outside of Chapel Hill where a fight is brewing between members of the community."

The camera moved from face to face, zoomed in and out. Ellis grinned. Nadean licked at a cold sore at the corner of her mouth. Woodrow studied the sky.

"Last month," Donna continued, "Bunce decided to landscape his front yard to resemble a south Pacific beach. While some residents of Oak Hills like Bunce's handiwork, a larger portion does not, and is pushing for the county commissioners to pass a building code that would mean the removal of the beach."

The camera turned from the beach, panning the neat yards and trim houses of the subdivision.

"Mr. Bunce," Donna said. "If the building code is passed, what do you plan to do?"

Woodrow stiffened his arms, staring at the tiny holes in the microphone thrust so close to his face. He glanced at Donna, opened his mouth, closed it, then stared at the sand. "I don't know."

Donna looked at Nadean. "Miss Tucker. If the building code is passed, do you plan to fight it?"

Nadean's knees felt weak, her heart pounded. She pressed once more at the strand of hair, then worked her fingers together. "Well, we . . . we hope it don't pass. We ain't trying to tell other people what to do on their land. Don't know why they try to tell us. It ain't like we making liquor or something." Nadean tongued her cold sore. "Yeah, we'll fight."

"Well," Donna continued, "do you think the problem here is simply the construction of your beach, or do you feel there is a larger social issue prompting the argument?"

Nadean nudged Woodrow with her elbow. Ellis reached and pulled the microphone close to his face. "Damn right, it's more than just that palm tree," he said. He hooked his fingers over the top of his belt. "It's a hell of a lot more."

"Ellis, what do you feel is the underlying problem?"

Ellis looked dead into the camera. "To start off, there's a bunch of high-class jackasses living around here," he explained. "They try to change everything." He pointed at a tree. "See that? That's a pecan tree. Pee-can. They say 'pa-con.'" Ellis hitched up his trousers. "And tell me this. How the hell does someone get two syllables out of o-i-l? It's oil, not 'oy-yul.'"

□   □   □

Mary giggled hysterically, and Jeffery was belly-laughing. They had already run the VCR back three times, and each time the interview seemed funnier.

"Woodrow needs to be holding a pitchfork," Jeffery said. "They would look like a New Wave version of *American Gothic.*"

"I know I shouldn't laugh at her," Mary said, "but it just kills me the way Nadean keeps trying to press down that sprig of hair."

On television, the beach looked even more colorful and bizarre than in real life—close-ups of the flamingos' heads, pebbles shining in the white sand, the palm's fronds contrasting against the backdrop of oaks. Ellis was bleeped so many times, his speech seemed beyond ridiculous. Already, five people had called to say they wanted to sign the petition.

Mary covered her mouth to stop giggling. The tape ended with Ellis standing ramrod straight, his jaw thrust forward, Nadean smiling, her tuft of stray hair waving like a flag, Woodrow staring at the sand, a final fade-out of the palm fronds stirred by a breeze.

While walking down the dirt road leading to the home place, Nadean recalled the last time she had traveled it in Jerome's car. Ahead, she could see the magnolia tree that scented the front yard, the clump of oaks that shaded the house. The top branches of the tallest one were splintered by lightning.

Nadean stood upon the road for several moments peering into the clump of trees. She had heard from her sister that the house was being torn down, but still the sight of the twisted lumber and piles of brick made her heart ache. She had always believed the airy rooms and squeaky porch boards were as permanent as the moon. In the backyard where she had lounged so many afternoons gazing into the clouds, the foundation of a new house was being staked out.

Nadean weaved through piles of rotting lumber to the old blackened hearth. The bricks were caked with the soot of thousands of fires, were as brittle as old bones. A skink sunned on top of the bricks, his blue tail vivid against the mortar and baked, orange clay. He blinked, then slipped into a crack.

"I ain't gonna hurt you, silly old lizard," Nadean said. "I remember your great-great-granddaddy running around these same bricks. Try as they might, couldn't none of my brothers catch him."

Nadean wiped away a layer of dirt covering the hearth and sat down. The bricks were warmed by the sun and reminded her of the old days, a crackling fire, the Dutch oven leaking the good-smelling steam of stewed beef and potatoes.

Ole cat used to lay here, she thought. Lazy damn thing he was. Would scratch you if you tried to move him. "Uncle" would lay here when he was too drunk to make it to bed. Which "uncle" was it—I forget—the one who lay here and let his hair catch a'fire? Many'a night I sit here while Mama rubbed Vicks on my chest trying to stop the croup. Felt good.

Nadean picked up one of the charred bricks, scratching the soot till red showed through. Mama would take some of this soot and mix it with kerosene, make me drink it when I had a cold. I'd cry and gag, but that stuff worked. Remember that night when the fireball rolled down the chimney during that bad, bad storm. Like to scared us all to death. How many times did I sit here and dress in the cold morning?

Nadean saw the lizard poke his head from the crack. "You the master of the house now, huh? Bet you think you bad, give the bugs and stuff 'round here pure hell. Well, you better haul yourself on down to the woods 'cause I think they're gonna be bulldozing this place right soon."

Nadean considered what she had said. Bulldoze it? Level even the bricks until the ground is smooth. Plant some new grass so there will just be a yard where a house once stood. New people walk over the top of the place I was born.

Nadean heard a truck slowing down, then saw a red Ford turn into the driveway. Two men stepped from the cab. They eyed Nadean while fastening carpenter's belts around their waists.

Ya'll can tear this place down if you like, she thought. Go ahead and level it clean and put up something new. Oak Hills will still be home to me, and I ain't gonna let nobody take that from me. People think they smarter than Nadean, but I'll show them. They want a fight; they ain't never seen fighting.

Nadean scooped up a handful of crumbled brick and dribbled it into her breast pocket. The red grains would blend nicely with the white sands of the beach.

The benches in the county commissioners' meeting room were full; against the back wall stood another couple dozen people. Mary and nearly one hundred supporters crowded the front of the room. Woodrow and twenty-three other people from Oak Hills sat in the rear benches. Reporters from every local paper filled the press bench.

The meeting began with the usual prayer. The first several items on the agenda consisted of county budget amendments and appointments. By the time the Oak Hills building code came up, the room was becoming stuffy and people were coughing and squirming in their seats.

"This hearing concerns a request for a building code from the Oak Hills community," chairman Clark began. "The floor is now open for debate."

Mary was quick to stand and ask for time at the podium. She introduced a series of speakers who came well prepared with facts and figures.

"Recent studies have shown that the projected completion of Interstate 40 could spark a twenty-five percent growth in our county," Dack argued. "If steps are not taken now to control this growth, the quality of life in Oak Hills that many of us have become accustomed to will rapidly deteriorate."

"What we are asking for is not an unusual request," Tom began. "Zoning and building codes are interpreted in various ways from community to community across the whole state. All we are asking is the right to decide the future face of our own community. What people do out of public sight with their property is their business. But, when something is constructed that is in view of the public, we feel it becomes everyone's business."

Mary's speakers had practiced their presentations until now they stood calmly and confidently before the commissioners, backs straight, eyes ahead, pronouncing each word as if it were a suture needed to close a great wound. They quoted local politicians, highway authorities, and other officials who were well versed in population and growth. Mary finished their argument by presenting the petition to chairman Clark, the list now containing ninety percent of the names of the residents of the subdivision.

A lull followed Mary's exit to her seat. The chairman studied the petition, looking up occasionally to scan faces in the crowd.

"Well, everything looks in order here, Mrs. Stewert," Clark said. "We'll now open the floor to those opposed to a building code."

Silence reigned except for low coughing. The people in Woodrow's group looked at one another. Most had never spoken before a group in their lives, especially the likes of county commissioners, lawyers, doctors, and people of education.

"You ask me, this whole thing smells like communism," Horace Tucker called out.

"That's right," Miss Penny said. "We never needed no building code before, and we don't need one now."

"I'd appreciate it if the people who wish to speak would come to the podium," Clark said.

Silence settled like a curtain again. Woodrow studied his fingernails, picking at the frayed edges of his cuticles. Twice people nudged him to talk, but each time he shook his head and sank lower.

Commissioner Canady cleared his throat. "Isn't there someone who would like to come up and tell us how you feel about Oak Hills staying the same? About how you want it to remain a free, peaceful country community?"

Mary turned in her seat and stared at the old-time residents. She smiled at their lowered faces, each breathing shallow as if in fear of being singled out. Finally, Bob Garner, the florist, stood and walked to the podium. He stood stiffly, arms pressed to his sides, and nodded briskly to the crowd before speaking.

"I reckon most of ya'll know me. I've run the florist shop for thirty-seven years. I was born in Oak Hills in a little house that used to stand out where the subdivision is now. It was torn down. I got a plot in the church cemetery waiting on me. It's right beside where my wife is buried." Garner cleared his throat and placed his hands on the podium. "Oak Hills, it's always been a good place to live, quiet, lots of trees, got the river to fish in or listen to. When I came back from the south Pacific, I decided right then I was staying the rest of my life. Actually, I reckon I decided that on Guam—if I got back. I remember lying there nights when things quieted down and picturing in my mind how the sun looked on Thunder Ridge late in the afternoon, how you could hear the rapids on Haw River when the water was up, how the doves sounded in the morning. Maybe that's why I bought into flowers, they seemed to fit so well with the life in Oak Hills."

Garner blinked hard, then adjusted his glasses where they had slid down the bridge of his nose. He looked directly at Mary. "I don't blame you new people for wanting to move here. You got an eye for the town just the same as me. All I'm asking is that you don't try and change the rules. We're adaptable people. We can go with the times. Miss Penny will tell you herself that she stopped using lard in her restaurant cooking. Uses vegetable oil now, ain't that right, Miss Penny?"

The old woman nodded.

"We can adapt to new ways," Garner continued. "They went and put in a record store right beside my florist shop. All day long I hear music coming through the wall—all that disco stuff and rock and roll. I asked the fellow who runs it to turn down the volume, and he did. The music don't much bother me now. We can adapt and get along. But we don't need laws to do that. All it takes is people talking, compromising some. That's the way we always done it here, and it's worked."

Garner opened his mouth to speak again, but then closed it as if he had decided he'd said enough. He nodded his head again, then returned to his seat. Silence descended again over the room. The commissioners stared at one another.

"Anyone else care to speak?" Clark said.

Ellis tried to stand, but Nadean grabbed his trouser pocket and held him down. Don't need another of his speeches, she thought. Her heart pounded harder and harder as the silence thickened, her mouth dry and bitter. Somebody else need to speak, else we gonna look mighty weak. Somebody got to, but God, oh, I can't get up there. I just can't.

Nadean felt curiously like she was out of body and floating above herself when she rose and began walking to the front of the room. The woman she followed grasped the podium with both hands, her legs shaking as if she were wet and cold.

Nadean looked with horror at the many faces fastened on her, none muted by cigarette smoke or hazed by dope in her veins. Her pulse was strong in her ears, her tongue glued in her mouth. "I ain't made no speech," she stammered. "I don't have no papers or nothing to read from." She stopped to breathe, felt dizzy for a moment, her throat seeming to close tighter and tighter as her eyes flicked from face to face. "But, I just want to talk—to talk to ya'll. Oak Hills is home." Nadean stopped and tried to swallow. She closed her eyes for a moment, hoping the dizziness would pass. She opened them to see Mary staring into her face, her arms crossed over her bosom. "Mary. Home used not to mean nothing to me, but it does now. We just want to live—to live as neighbors with ya'll. We just want—we want—to be friends."

Mary diverted her gaze. Nadean stared at the old-timers of Oak Hills. "In some ways, I don't deserve to be talking up here," Nadean said. "Mr. Garner, he off fighting a war and dreaming of coming back here. Me, I run off first chance I got thinking everything made of gold outside of Oak Hills. Thought I didn't never want to see a tobacco plant or Haw River again. Lord, I was wrong about things. *Lord,* I was."

Nadean wiped a trickle of sweat from her brow. "I did a lot of things up north I'm 'shamed of."

Several people sitting in Mary's group snickered. Nadean swallowed hard and continued. "I did things I was taught was wrong, but I thought the rules didn't matter no more."

"That's why we're asking for rules now," a man called out from Mary's group. "It's evident you don't think rules matter."

Nadean looked at the man. "No, I've learned a lot, mister. More than you could know. People here in Oak Hills gave me a second chance. The last thing now I want to do is bother people."

Nadean stared at her hands, then at Woodrow. "That youngun falling in the pool the other night scared me. Woodrow said he can build a fence, a big one, higher than his head, one no youngun can climb over. Build it out of hog wire so folks could still see in, but the pool be safe."

"Who wants to see in?" someone called out.

Several people laughed.

"Hog wire seems appropriate," another person said. "Hog wire to surround a pigsty."

More laughter.

Mary turned and asked her people to be quiet. "Nadean," she said. "You just can't seem to understand. The pool is ugly. *Ugly.* Not only is it unsafe, but no one wants to look at it."

"You can't speak for everyone," Garner called out.

"I like it," another of the old-timers shouted.

Clark pounded on his desk and asked for order.

Nadean gripped the podium till her knuckles hurt. "We'll build a wood fence, then," she pleaded. "A rock fence if you ask for it."

"It would have to be fifty feet high," someone shouted.

Nadean blinked back tears. "We all got things that matter to us. Mr. Garner got his flowers. Woodrow got his hounds. Mary, you got them pretty fish in your house. Shelby and Dick, ya'll care a bunch 'bout them eagles out where you sail your boat. Everybody got different habits and interests, and there ain't no reason we can't compromise some and get along. I know one thing we all share. Oak Hills is home and that means something. Some of us been here all along, some of us new, and me, I finally wised up just in time. But we all know it a special place. We all found our home."

Nadean tried to think of something else to say, but it wouldn't come. "Thank you," she stammered and hurried to her seat. Mary stared at her hands. Commissioner Canady watched her, a smile covering his face.

An murmur rolled through the crowd. Mack Lupo, standing against the back wall, stepped forward into the aisle. "I got something to say," he began. He had been drinking heavily, his words thick with alcohol. "I got something to say, but I ain't gonna say it like the last two." He blinked hard, then thrust out his chin. "I don't like you new people. You come in here buying up the land and making taxes go up, cutting down all the trees. You got no right."

Several of the old-timers motioned and hissed for Mack to sit down. He ignored them.

"I've lived here all my life except when I went to Vietnam—probably when most of ya'll were hiding out in college or in Canada. Most of you in the subdivision been here a year or less, and now you're trying to rule the place, getting all your buddies to move down from New Jersey or California or some other place you've screwed up. I wish you'd go the hell on back."

Commissioner Canady raised one arm. "Son, you're not helping your cause none by using such language."

Mack sneered. "You got a lot of room to talk, Canady, sitting up there in your big chair. All the building going on in this county helps out your store. Every new house means more money for you."

Canady's eyes glinted cold.

"I'll leave it like this," Mack said. "Me and my brothers still own seventy-six acres in Oak Hills. We ain't selling out like the Bunces. I catch any of you newcomers on my pasture with your pretty picnic baskets and fancy wine, or walking around with your butterfly nets, I'm whipping ass. Any of your fancy dogs cross my line, I'm shooting it. Hear me? You better take it serious."

Mack turned and walked from the room, glaring at Benson Bunce, who sat at the end of a bench. The room was silent. Finally, Benson heaved to his feet and walked slowly to the front of the room. Sweat glistened on his forehead and his voice trembled as he began to speak.

"Well, I didn't come here with a speech either, but I guess a lot of this trouble has come from me so I ought to say something." Benson paused to catch his breath, studying the faces of the commissioners. "Where that subdivision is now, used to be fine farming land and forest. Nearly all of it belonged to me and my brothers. Close to a couple hundred acres. I can remember when there wasn't fifty houses in all of Oak Hills, and now I bet there's been a hundred built in the past couple years. It reminds me of Carrboro, how it used to be a pretty little place, was quiet and all, and now when school's in, you can't even cross the street."

Benson paused to pull a handkerchief from his shirt pocket. He mopped his forehead. "I'm not going to ask you commissioners not to pass this building code, because I can already see it will. I guess, too, that a man who decided to sell off land his grandpa sweated to buy has sold his right to complain, too. I got a fair price for that land."

Benson half turned so he was facing Woodrow's small band. "I guess what bothers me most is that the people I grew up with are going to pay for my greed. All my brother ever wanted to do was make something pretty. Something that looked different. But I guess this ain't the time and age to act different. People ain't comfortable with it."

Benson sighed and hunched his shoulders. "Hell, I'm talking like a fool up here. That's all I got to say."

Benson stomped from the meeting room. The building code was passed by a vote of four to one.

16

reakfast was silent at Woodrow's table the following morning. Ellis divided his grits into small piles, stirred them together, added more butter and salt. Nadean sipped her coffee. Woodrow chomped loudly on bacon that had been overcooked. A rap on the door caused all three to jump in their chairs. Nadean glanced at Woodrow, then hurried to open it.

"Who in the world be knocking this time'a morning?" she asked.

Deputy Franklin Smith, Miss Penny's nephew, stood outside holding his hat in one hand. In the other hand he held a folded paper. "Sorry to bother ya'll, ma'am," he said. "But I need to speak to Woodrow."

Nadean called, so Woodrow pushed from the table and walked out on the porch.

"Sorry to bother you so early in the morning, Mr. Bunce," Franklin said, "but I was driving by and saw the curtains open."

"What you need?" Woodrow asked.

Franklin cleared his throat. He unfolded the paper and stared at it for several seconds. "Mr. Bunce, I hate to have to be the one doing this, but there was a complaint made last night about your yard. You know with the new building code."

"Building code?" Nadean hissed. "That damn thing was just passed last night."

Franklin raised one hand. "I know it, but it's already in the book." He nodded toward the subdivision. "Those folks act fast." He handed the paper to Woodrow. "Mr. Bunce, I have to give you this summons asking that you appear in court."

"Court?"

"Yeah, a week from today. But, if you cut down the palm tree and put up a fence around your pool before then, the charges will be dropped."

Franklin looked over his shoulder, paused, then spoke in a lower voice. "Mr. Bunce, I'll tell you something, but you can't tell no one I said it."

Woodrow nodded.

"If you don't cut the tree down, the fine is only twenty-five dollars. You could even appeal that, and keep this thing tied up in court for months. A good lawyer might make it a year. You never know how things might change in a year."

Franklin took two steps backwards. "Well, you have the subpoena. I had to bring it. Sorry to have bothered you so early."

Nadean and Woodrow watched the patrol car until it was out of sight. "Woodrow," Nadean said. "I'll pay that twenty-five dollars myself, even if I have to get down on my knees and scrub floors."

The palm fronds still swayed as high as ever a week later when Woodrow stood before the district court judge. Under the urging of Benson, Porter Bunce had agreed to handle the case for Woodrow. The court was full of traffic offenders, and the judge wasted no time in fining Woodrow, then accepting Porter's request that the sentence be appealed. Woodrow was barely out of the courthouse when Mary Stewert's telephone began ringing.

Benson knew the house was long empty before the squealing door was half open. Reba wouldn't have let a door squeal for two minutes. He hesitated, peering into the gloom of the living room.

No glow shone from the small porcelain lamp that had sat on the mantel, the flying ducks painted on the shade, no odor of wood smoke or pork frying, no "Well my God, Benson. You finally decide to wander by again?"

The house was beyond dead, for even the carcass of an animal kept its shape and smell and color for a number of days. This was not the house he had often visited, now only bare rooms, weak sunlight filtering through dusty shades, a lingering odor of mildew and mold.

Benson circled the room, then walked cautiously into the next room. He scouted the corners, but there were no ghosts to haunt him—even the spirits in the house having departed. He could not remember exactly where the table had sat; so many nights he had rested there eating a plate of fresh butter beans and ham, washing it down with cold, iced tea. A ceramic crock had rested on the shelf, kept ready with bourbon whiskey to be drunk straight from a water glass.

Benson entered the small bedroom in the rear of the house. Something moved—a flutter and squeal—but the ghost proved to be only a screech owl hurtling into a wall, rebounding to the floor, then escaping through a busted windowpane. Draped along the windowsill, Benson spied the shed skin of a large rat snake.

Hadn't the bed been under that window?—a single mattress so narrow we were always hugging. I used to rise up on one elbow and watch the moon rising over the ridgeline. Yeah, and that scar in the floorboards we made the night we broke the bed frame. I can barely see it now, packed full of dust.

On a bare shelf, Benson spied a postcard. He lifted the yellowed, curled card and looked at the picture. Delta land, cypress trees growing from mossy water, some kind of long-legged bird perched on a log.

He turned the card over, saw poor handwriting, "Come on down, Curtis," scrawled in big letters. Who the hell is Curtis?

Benson dropped the card, watched it flip like a broken wing before settling with a puff of dust. Where'd she meet this Curtis fellow? Is that where she went? He unzipped his fly and inserted his hand in his trousers, gently fingering the knot on his testicle. Yep, no denying it, the damn thing was bigger than a week ago. Had been getting bigger and bigger for weeks now. He could admit that to himself in this vacant house where life had stopped and there was no future to prompt his denial. Yeah, it's getting bigger. Hard, too, like a damn acorn. Liable to be fucking cancer. Might be.

Benson knew the sunlight would shrink the knot once he was outside again and he would deny any possibility of illness. Margo's kiss when he got home would shrink it, as would a cold beer or a hot buttermilk bisquit filled with butter and molasses. But standing here in this gloomy, dank room where even death was more tangible than nothingness, he could face the possibility that he might die, could admit to himself that life had become so mundane and boring that even a fight with cancer might be relief.

Benson zipped his trousers. Curtis? No, she didn't have a brother named Curtis. He's just some man that had more balls than me.

The front door squealed again as Benson closed it. He blinked in the strong sunlight, breathed fresh air, felt the knot immediately shrink to half its size. He opened a pint of Old Crow bourbon and drank down straight an amount equal to half a water glass, grimacing as his stomach burned.

"Ugly damn shack here," he said aloud. "Uglier than a damn boil."

Taking a book of matches from his pocket, Benson reached through the shattered windowpane and lit the edge of the parched shade. It flared as if soaked in kerosene. The house quickly burned to ashes.

Nancy was at her beauty parlor, the kids still at school, when Mack Lupo called his brothers on the c.b. radio and asked them to stop plowing and meet him at his house. They sat on the front porch so as not to track mud into the house, sipping beer that Mack supplied.

"I hear you raised some hell at that meeting the other night," Wayne said.

"I didn't say nothing except what a lot of other people around here wanted to say. I just had the guts." Mack lit a cigarette. He drew the smoke in carefully, his blue eyes trained on his brothers, who sat side by side in the porch swing. "So, what you two decided?"

The young men exchanged glances. Wayne folded his arms,

then sighed. He looked his older brother in the eye. "Shit, Mack. One more year, that's it. We'll go for a big one. I just hope the hell we ain't hanging ourself."

Mack's eyes crinkled at the edges as he fought back a smile. "Shit. We ain't never come close to getting busted. Hell, I do the running." He flicked his partially burned cigarette from the porch. "All right, we got a deal. The last year. We'll plant 'bout two hundred sets and see what takes. Make a wad and get out. Hell, I might just go to the technical school, too. Lupo Brothers Heating and Air. I like the sound of it."

Mack turned up his beer. "Now what we have to worry about is if they try to clear the ridge before next fall. We need to slow down the building a notch or two."

"How the hell are we going to do that?" Bill asked. "They're building houses 'round here quicker than shit through a goose."

Mack smiled again. "You boys seem to be forgetting that big brother here is trained in guerrilla warfare tactics. Bulldozers don't run too well with sugar in the gas tanks." Mack set his empty can on the floor. "But first, I think we ought to use some of their tactics. Them yuppies, or whatever the hell they are."

"What's that?" Wayne asked.

"Remember how they got that TV crew out to Woodrow's place? Made the beach look like some damn freak show. That got a lot of people on their side."

"Well, how can that help us?" Bill asked.

"Contractors don't bulldoze new lots if they don't have people wanting houses." Mack lit another cigarette. "What if we were to start painting a different picture of Oak Hills? Start making a lot of noise around here at night. A little spray-paint graffiti on some of them pretty houses. Maybe a little herbicide on a few fancy lawns. Wouldn't take but a phone call to have the news people swarming over this place. Whispering Pines subdivision suddenly wouldn't look like such a paradise."

Bill and Wayne grinned. "Sounds like fun," Wayne said, "but we could get in a lot of trouble, too. People ain't going to take kindly to someone spray-painting their houses."

"Just leave the planning to me," Mack said. "I got night eyes. That's what they told me in Nam."

Ellis decided to take the long way home from school, walking the route that led by the boys' home. He had avoided the Home since moving out and did not understand why now he chose that route except that the sun was warm and the dogwoods were in bloom. He slowed his pace in front of the Home.

All of the boys were inside, forced to study that first hour after school. Only a few hopping robins populated the long front lawn. Ellis recalled a spanking he had received once for killing a robin with a slingshot. He studied the figures he could see moving inside the squat, white dorms.

Little suck-asses studying in there like professors, he thought. Me, I study when I feel like it. Don't study if I don't feel like it.

He heard the distant whine of an airplane. He spied the plane in high clouds, sunlight glinting off one wing as it flew west. He wished he were on the airplane and hadn't listened to Woodrow.

This damn town is getting crazier and crazier. I've never seen such fussing and cussing in all my life. Liable to be a civil war in here by next week.

Through the windows of the dorm, Ellis watched the shapes moving. I wonder who's sleeping in my bunk. Some little pisser. Lying there studying his ABCs right now. Scared shitless of Enzor. I wonder if he scratched my name off the bed frame?

Ellis thrust out his bottom lip and shook his head. I don't give a shit if he scratched off my name. I don't give a shit for that whole place—bunk, Enzor, and bullshit. The first time a man starts worrying about a home, planting grass, planting God damn watermelons, he's the first step toward the loony bin and the grave. Me, I'll just keep my feet moving and live forever.

Ellis turned from the dorms and continued on his way, sighting on a cloud floating westward above the oaks.

Benson parked at the curb in front of Woodrow's house, then slowly climbed the hill. He stopped at the edge of the beach and leaned to lift a handful of sand, letting it trickle between his fingers. From the corner of his eye, he saw Nadean rise from her chair on the porch and stand by the railing.

A damn sight, ain't it, he thought. I can't believe that tree is still living.

Benson slowly climbed the porch steps, extending his hand when Woodrow met him. "Evening, brother," Benson said. Nadean went into the house and came out with another chair. "Hello, Nadean," he said, tipping his brimmed cap.

"Won't you sit down?" Nadean offered.

Benson hitched both trouser legs and settled into the chair. He folded his arms.

"We appreciate you speaking up at the hearing," Nadean said. She wondered why he was here now, if he was bringing more bad news.

"Well, me speaking up didn't do any good." Benson unfolded his arms and looked at his watch. "The president could have spoken and it wouldn't have done any good."

Woodrow sat ramrod straight in his chair. He twirled tiny swirls in the black hair covering his wrist. Benson looked him in the eye for a moment, wet his lips, and leaned forward.

"Woodrow. Nadean. I know things haven't been too good between us lately. And, I reckon if I'm fair about it, the fault has mostly been with me. I'd like to patch things up if ya'll feel we can?"

Woodrow nodded and smiled. Nadean pushed to the edge of her chair. "Lord, Benson, we ain't the type to stay mad with people."

"Well, I'm sorry about the whole thing," Benson answered. "I know Porter is, too. These days, if a man ain't right with his family, there's no one he can trust in."

"We're sorry, too," Nadean said. "Ain't we, Woodrow?"

Woodrow cleared his throat. "I ain't never been mad."

Benson stood and walked to the porch railing. He stared at the beach. "Woodrow, we can keep this building code on appeal for a while, but not forever. Sooner or later, it's going to come to you cutting that palm tree down and putting up a fence."

"But, that deputy said folks' minds might change after a spell," Nadean said. "After they get used to it. He said—"

"People's minds ain't going to change," Benson interrupted. "Unless they change for the worst." He swept his arm in an arc, eclipsing the beach, the neat homes of the subdivision. "That's Oak Hills out there now. That's reality. Woodrow, I heard today that Consolidated Paper is selling their timberland to the realty company. That's most of the ridge where you run your dogs. I bet you in five years that ridge will be as crowded as around here."

Woodrow looked from his brother to the forest that covered the highland above the subdivision. "This is home, Ben. I got no place else."

Benson chewed at a raw spot on his bottom lip. His head was beginning to throb from the aftereffects of the pint of whiskey he'd guzzled. He took a deep breath, only then making up his mind. "No, this ain't the only place," Benson said. "I've been doing some thinking today, Woodrow. I miss farming, and wish to hell I hadn't sold out to those developers. But farming is dead around here, anyway. This ain't farmland no longer."

Benson took two steps closer to Woodrow. "What if I was to

buy some land, maybe about fifty acres, somewhere farther south.
Down in South Carolina, maybe Georgia. Land that ain't
crowded. Good for growing sweet potatoes or something that
would just need planting and tending and could be harvested
with migrant help." Benson stopped to suck another deep breath.
"Woodrow, what would you and Nadean say to coming down
and running the place for me?"

Nadean gave a small cry of surprise. Woodrow furrowed his
brow and closed his fingers into fists. "I don't know nothing
about growing sweet potatoes."

"Sweet potatoes. Hell, watermelons. I know you can grow
them. It wouldn't matter what you decided to grow. Ya'll would
run the place. I'd come down when I could, help out, we'd split
the profits. If I bought land far enough south, you could have a
hundred palm trees."

"I never lived no place but Oak Hills," Woodrow answered.

"But this ain't Oak Hills no longer," Benson said. "Our hills
are dead, little brother."

Benson turned and shouted into the air. His cry echoed off the
walls of the nearest house, then a further one. One of the hounds
bayed. "See what this place has become? Woodrow, I could buy
land where you could run your dogs all night and not once cross a
road. Not see a single porch light."

Woodrow took his time, but he smiled, the creases in his
cheeks pulling his forehead smooth.

"Wouldn't be no damn building code down there," Benson
continued. "Woodrow, have you noticed there are no frogs
chirping this spring? They've left. Used to be thousands around
here, but they've all gone."

Woodrow cocked his head and listened. A car door across the
way slammed, the low strains of a stereo leaked from an open
window.

"Ya'll just think about it," Benson said. "Give it a lot of

thought. Things ain't never going to be the same again around here. But if we went south, who knows?"

"It makes me just furious," Mary said to the group of neighbors gathered on her front porch. "We've approached this the fair way, gotten the support of the community, went through legal channels, and Bunce still won't comply." She stomped her foot in anger. "What do we do next?"

"What *do* we do?" Jeffery asked William Bates, the lawyer.

Bill screwed up the side of his mouth and looked at his feet, then back at Jeffery. "Well, not much. Like you said, Mary, we went through legal channels, and that is what Bunce is doing now. He's been charged with disobeying the building code and has the right to appeal."

"Well, how long can he appeal?" Mary shouted.

"Porter Bunce is handling this. He ain't no slouch. He could drag this on for months—maybe up to a year."

A round of sighs and moans went up from the crowd. As they quieted, music was heard, growing louder by the second.

"What in the world is that?" Shelby asked.

Through the entrance to Whispering Pines, a pickup turned in, music blasting from a loudspeaker mounted on top of the cab. The driver drove slowly. The music was so loud it was hard to distinguish, but as the truck neared Mary's house, she recognized it as Hank Williams, Jr., singing "A Country Boy Can Survive"—a man and song she had always detested. Everyone stared in disbelief as the truck passed, the driver waving while cranking up the stereo a notch higher. Everyone chattered as they listened to the truck wind through the subdivision. No sooner did it reach the far side of the community, when another truck turned into the entrance, a similar mindless song blasting from the speakers.

The parade included a third truck that even stopped in front of Mary's house, revved its engine, then burned rubber for fifty feet. Mary put her hands over her ears. "We should call the police," she shouted above the din.

"Who were they?" Dack asked when the last truck exited the subdivision, promptly turning off the music.

"I know I've seen that first truck before," Jeffery said. "I believe I've seen it at one of Woodrow's parties."

Mary had been sick most mornings with her pregnancy, and now she felt nausea rising again. She excused herself and went inside to lie down.

The next morning, three residents in the subdivision awoke to find graffiti spray-painted in red across the front of their houses. "Go Home Damn Yankees," "Get the Hell Back North," "No More Yuppies," and other slogans were written in tall letters. Franklin Smith investigated for the sheriff's department, but told the residents that nothing could be done unless the culprit was caught in the act. Again that afternoon, vehicles circled through the subdivision playing loud music. This time, six cars circled, all driven by young men. Each turned the music off promptly upon leaving the subdivision.

The next morning, Mary suffered her usual nausea upon getting out of bed. Finally, she felt able to walk into the living room and open the drapes. She stared outside at the bright morning, her eyes narrowing as she realized something looked wrong with the yard. "Jeffery, come here," she called. When he came from the kitchen, she pointed at the lawn. "What's wrong with the grass?"

Jeffery leaned toward the window. Without answering, he walked outside to the middle of the front yard. When he returned after several minutes, his face was a mix of wonder and anger. "The grass looks like it's dying in patches. It looks very strange and wilted."

The previous fall, they had spent nearly a thousand dollars having the yard landscaped and planted with winter rye. A green winter lawn was common in Whispering Pines. By midday, word spread through the subdivision that nearly a dozen homes had the same problem with either their grass or their shrubbery. Dack called the county extension office. A man was sent out, who, upon studying the first yard, announced that someone had sprayed the lawns with a common farm herbicide. That night, two more houses were spray-painted. The next night, three more lawns were doused with herbicide.

"The controversy that has surrounded the community of Oak Hills in southern Orange County has erupted again," announced the anchorman that afternoon on the six o'clock news. The screen flashed a film showing houses in Whispering Pines being painted or sandblasted to remove graffiti, panned manicured lawns that were zebra-striped with dead grass, azalea bushes wilted and dying. Several homeowners were interviewed, and said they were shocked and angered by the senseless vandalism. "At this time, law authorities have no suspects," the announcer concluded.

Mary and Jeffery stared at the television until the film ended. Mary stood and clicked off the set. "Well, there's no doubt in my mind who's behind this," she hissed. "Woodrow and Nadean know who's doing this. They may be doing it themselves out of spite."

Jeffery shook his head. "I really don't think Woodrow or Nadean would do this, Mary. Not them. It's someone in Oak Hills, I'm sure of that. Some redneck. I've got a good suspect, but no way to prove it. But, it's not Woodrow or Nadean."

"Well, I bet they know who is doing this," Mary shrieked. "I tell you, Jeffery. Nadean is conniving. I've learned that. Woodrow's just simpleminded, but Nadean is conniving. I know she's the one that had Woodrow appeal. I know it, and I think she's behind this vandalism."

"Sit down, Mary," Jeffery said. "Just sit down and take a deep breath and get control of yourself. The doctor has already said your blood pressure is too high."

Mary's hand instinctively went to her belly. She sat back down, then took several deep breaths. "I'm calm, Jeffery. I'm fine." She breathed deeply again. "But, we can't sit by and let our neighborhood be destroyed. I've already heard the Lawsons say they are considering selling and moving closer to Chapel Hill. If this stupidity doesn't stop immediately, I want us to go en masse to Woodrow's house and confront them. They have got to see that we are serious, that we're not going to be pushed around. This is my home."

During the night, Mary and Jeffery were jerked from sleep by an explosion. Standing barefoot on their front lawn, joined by several neighbors, they stared at the splintered remains of their mailbox and post. Next morning, a detective decided it had been destroyed by a half stick of dynamite.

Nadean and Woodrow were as disturbed by the vandalism as anyone in the subdivision, and as to who was behind it. Although most of the townspeople were against the building code, neither of them could imagine anyone who would resort to such acts. Actually, Ellis thought the night raids to be daring, and at worst, just revenge for how Woodrow and Nadean had been treated. He even wished he could participate. Nadean sensed this, and made sure to see he was in bed and asleep before she retired. Any suspicion she had of him being involved was laid to rest when, in the middle of the night, the explosion in the Stewerts' yard gathered the three of them at the front door.

The following morning was Saturday, and they were eating a late breakfast when voices were heard outside, then steps coming across the porch. Nadean opened the front door, then took a step backwards when she saw at least a dozen people from the subdivision standing there, Mary foremost.

Nadean nodded, then looked over her shoulder at Woodrow. "What can I do for ya'll?" she asked.

Jeffery stood behind Mary, his hand resting on her shoulder. Nadean searched the crowd, recognized Dack and Shelby and Sue and Paul and several other people from the parties.

"Nadean," Mary began, "we've called the State Bureau of Investigation and asked that they have the proper authorities investigate what happened last night. A destroyed mailbox is serious business."

"What mailbox?" Nadean asked. Woodrow rose from the table, followed by Ellis.

"Our mailbox that was destroyed by dynamite last night," Mary said coldly. "Nadean." Mary shifted her glance to Woodrow, who towered over the small woman. "Woodrow. I want you to know that if you have anything to do with this violence, you better come clean. When someone is caught—and they will be caught—we will prosecute to the full extent of the law. Believe me."

Nadean turned to Woodrow, her mouth open with surprise. "You better wait a minute there, Mary," Nadean said. "You think me or Woodrow or Ellis have anything to do with this, you barking up the wrong tree, honey. I know we got our differences, but this stuff ain't nothing to do with us."

"Frankly, I think you're lying," Mary said.

"Don't you call her a liar," Ellis said, stepping forward. "You damn . . . you damn . . ."

Woodrow clamped his hand over Ellis's mouth and pulled him back. "We got nothing to do with this trouble. Ya'll are wrong."

"Woodrow," Jeffery said, "we don't actually think you or

Nadean or Ellis are causing the trouble—I don't—but I feel you must know who is doing it. That was dynamite last night. Sooner or later, someone is going to get hurt. If you know who's doing it, you've got to stop them."

"Well, I tell you what, Jeffery," Nadean said. "We don't know who is doing it, no more than that palm tree does. But I tell ya'll this. Ya'll started all the trouble, making laws and things that weren't never here before. If there's trouble, looks to me like it been brought upon yourself."

"Damn right," said Ellis, having escaped Woodrow's grasp.

"Well, we'll tell you what," Mary began. "The state patrol has pledged to start patrolling this neighborhood until this stupidity stops. And when someone is caught, they'll wish they never set a foot in my yard. I promise you that."

"You're talking mighty tough," Ellis said, "seeing that you have half the subdivision standing behind you on the porch."

"We've come en masse to show we're standing together," Mary retorted. "And while we're here, I just want to remind you, that palm will come down. It's law, Woodrow. You can fight it, but the people of this community will win."

"It'll be over my dead body," Nadean said.

"Mine, too," Ellis said.

"Ya'll got no right coming here. Ya'll . . ." Nadean's voice broke into a sob.

Woodrow stepped between Nadean and the people on the porch. His hands trembled at his sides. "I'm tired of this. All this arguing and fighting. It ain't right. I want you all to leave from here."

No one had ever seen Woodrow display anger, and the sight of his hands trembling, his face colored red, made each take a step back. "Woodrow," Mary stammered, "we're not . . ."

"I want you to leave from here," Woodrow boomed.

Jeffery pulled Mary by her shoulder toward the steps. She

opened her mouth to speak again, but her words froze. The group
started down the hill, skirting the beach, mumbling and looking
back.

"Assholes," Ellis shouted.

17

he oak trees budded in clusters of pale green leaves that shaded wisteria vines climbing fence posts. Birds scavenged the countryside for nesting material, while Miss Penny chopped down her collard stalks and tilled the soil for snow peas and spinach. The fronds of the palm were stirred by warming breezes as April slipped into the bright dress of May.

But as Oak Hills moved into another season of birth and renewal, the fight between the townspeople and residents of the subdivision grew harsher and more bitter. The coalition met several times to discuss ways of hurrying Woodrow's appeal through court; the townspeople began collecting money in a gallon pickle jar to aid Woodrow's defense. When members of the two factions met, usually they passed without even a nod. Sales in the local stores dropped considerably as the subdivision residents carried their business to Chapel Hill or Durham. In retaliation, many of the townspeople who would never before have thought of being inconsiderate began mimicking the teen-agers by driving through the subdivision in the peaceful early evening with their radios blaring, or walking their dogs in the neighborhood and allowing them to soil the pretty yards. The vandalism continued.

At least twice a week, a house was spray-painted. Several more mailboxes were blown up. Two bulldozers left on the ridge over-night were doused with gasoline and burned. The local news kept up with the problems, and reported that close to fifty thousand dollars' worth of insurance claims had been filed. And for the first time in a year and a half, a week passed without the sale of a new lot in the subdivision.

The state patrol and sheriff's department patrolled the subdivision at night, but no one was ever caught. Whoever made the trouble slipped in and out as silently as clouds of fog.

Mack Lupo squatted in the humid air of the greenhouse where they once had grown tomatoes. Using a spray bottle, he carefully watered the small marijuana plants growing in foot tubs. Bill and Wayne helped him.

"Two more weeks, we can set them," Mack said. "They look good, too—a shitload of females."

"You ain't scared we're wasting our time?" Bill asked. "You really think they're going to hold off cutting into the ridge?"

"Oh, they'll cut in a little, but not far enough up to bother us. We'll harvest this little crop, boys."

Bill and Wayne had stopped going out with Mack at night. The first few times had been fun, but when Mack started using the dynamite they used to blow stumps, things got too serious.

"Well, if we've slowed them down that much, don't you reckon it's time to quit fucking with their houses?" Wayne asked. "There ain't no sense in pushing your luck."

Mack smiled. He liked the fear and frustration he saw in the new people's eyes, how a two-dollar can of spray paint could lift several thousand dollars from their checking accounts. He remembered when he came home from boot camp, his hair cropped short, students in Chapel Hill laughed at him, made snide remarks, even called him murderer or baby killer. He remembered vividly when he returned from the war, how people were protesting on Franklin Street. Once in Breadman's restaurant a table of students got up and left when he sat down at the next table and they spied his Airborne tattoo. These new people in the subdivision were just grown-up students, and he liked getting a little revenge.

"Oh, I'm just having a little fun with them," Mack said. "I'll start easing off. Hell, I ain't the only person messing with them now. Looks like it's become a community project. I saw old man Smith riding through there the other night, his radio turned up loud. Saw him throw out a Pepsi can, too."

"Well, let them do it then," Bill said. "The last thing we need is you getting caught. Let's plant this dope, pray we don't get busted, and move on."

Mack smiled again. He watched spray bead on the tiny leaves, then trickle down.

A late cold snap settled over Oak Hills one afternoon in the second week of May. Gardeners were warned to cover young plants. Woodrow stood on his porch in the twilight, breathing fragrant cold air from Canada. Finally, he turned and went inside to dress for one last hunt before summer.

"Oh, Woodrow, you ain't going hunting again, are you?" Nadean protested. "I thought you were finished till next fall."

"The weatherman said it's going down to thirty-five tonight."

"You ought to stay in here and get some sleep. I thought you said you were gonna plant melons tomorrow."

"I am. I'm going to hunt tonight, too."

Nadean knew it was useless to argue with Woodrow, but she dreaded being alone with her thoughts. During the past couple of weeks she had clung to his back in bed even on warm nights. She dreamed as soon as her eyes closed, jumbled, disturbing dreams— dogs clawed at the windows; the palm dropped her coconuts and grew lidless, blue eyes; eagles swooped down and clawed off the palm fronds; her mother stood at the foot of the bed and warned her to leave.

And when she was awake, she had to endure the silent phone calls, now at least three times a day. Cars slowed in front of the house, then peeled rubber. Several times someone had strewn trash across the beach during the night. And now Woodrow was wanting to leave her alone again and let his hounds bay from the top of the ridge.

Nadean watched Woodrow draw tight the thick laces on his boots. She also worried about him. He sat for long periods now, staring from the porch toward the houses of the subdivision. His eating had fallen off, and she feared the strain of knowing how the beach had rent the community was tearing at him. Several times she had opened her mouth to ask him shouldn't they cut the palm, but the words wouldn't come.

Nadean leaped in her chair when someone rapped on the front door, but it was only Benson, who let himself in and walked, smiling, across the floor.

"I just flew in an hour ago," he began. "Been down in Mississippi visiting a realtor. Woodrow, I looked at a small farm. It's perfect. Exactly what I've been looking for."

Woodrow finished lacing his boot, then began on the other one. "How many acres?"

"Seventy-two. Sixty of it tillable. There's even a ten-acre rice field."

Benson talked fast as he told of the land, described the black, loamy soil, cypress swamps abundant with reed thickets and alligators, the strange accent of the locals, a dark-skinned people with mixed Indian blood, the cluster of orange trees growing behind the four-room frame house.

"The house needs a little work, but that won't be any problem," Benson continued. "I could add a room or two, fix it up real nice. And the land, Woodrow, you gotta see it. Ain't another house for miles. You could run your hounds till you're blue in the face."

Nadean rose from her chair and stood beside the two men. When Benson first proposed moving, she had been skeptical, but lately with the harassment they were receiving, the idea sounded better and better. She rocked her weight from heel to toe. "What's the weather like, Benson? It warm down there?"

"Warm as toast almost the whole year. Good rainfall. The man told me he's seen watermelons grown there big as a wheelbarrow. Ya'll need to come down and look at it."

Ellis had been listening from his room, but at the mention of travel, came running. "You said there are alligators down there? Big ones?"

"Full grown. I saw one in a pond that looked like a log."

"I'd like to see a live alligator," Ellis answered.

Woodrow finished lacing his boots, then began rolling his trouser legs to the top of the leather. Everyone watched him work. "What do you think?" Benson asked. "Don't you think we ought to ride down there for a couple of days? Get a feel for the place?"

"I'll go," Ellis said.

"I'd like to see it, too," Nadean said softly.

Woodrow lifted his flashlight from the table. He clicked on the beam and shone it against the wall. "I ain't never lived no place else."

"Just come with me and look at it," Benson argued. "That's all I ask."

Woodrow slipped the long silver flashlight into his trouser pocket. "When you out of school, boy?" he asked Ellis.

"Sixteen days."

"We might ride down there then and take a look."

A smile circled the room. Nadean envisioned a field with watermelons so large only Woodrow could lift them, a land of peace dotted with swaying palms that swept to the horizon.

Mary was scraping food from the dishes before slipping them into the washer. She was annoyed that again Jeffery had to work late, said it might take as long as midnight. He won't eat when he gets home, she lamented. Just fall right into bed and go to sleep. I wish sometimes he hadn't even gotten that promotion.

Mary reached and wiped a trickle of tears from her eyes. Lately, she seemed to cry over the smallest problem, felt sick every morning. Was she going to be sick and upset for the next six months?

She also was having trouble sleeping. She couldn't remember sleeping really well since Woodrow appealed his violation of the building code. How could he do that? Just decide that he didn't want to abide by the law and the hell with everyone else. People were supposed to obey laws. The community had voiced a majority opinion, and now a crazy farmer and his whore didn't want to go along. She was also infuriated by the vandalism, the parade of noisy cars in the evening. At night, she kept her shades drawn tight, fearful that someone watched from the darkness.

Mary often dreamed of palm trees. She dreamed that all the oak trees had changed into palms except for a single oak in her front yard. She clung to the oak's trunk, but the palms grew taller and taller, choking off all sunlight below. She dreamed that her child was born, but she unwrapped the blanket to find she held only a coconut. She dreamed that during dinner a palm tree grew up from the bowl of ambrosia.

And if she wasn't dreaming of palm trees, she dreamed other weird, distorted things. She was a student again in journalism school and her professor was a black child who made her stand with her nose against the blackboard. She dreamed a moose was eating the plants in the den. She dreamed she stood in the front yard washing diapers in a bucket of cold water, watching Nadean pass wearing a backpack. Nadean turned and gazed at her with pity but continued on her way. The dreams twisted her sleep and caused her to awaken and lay for hours looking at the ceiling and wishing for morning.

Mary held a glass closer to the lamp over the sink, inspecting a chip in the rim. "Oh, damn. Another of my good crystals." She studied the small imperfection, wondering if Jeffery might sand it out. Suddenly she realized how silly it was to worry over a glass. Was her whole life turning into morning sickness and the plight of her dinnerware? Mary stopped and took a deep breath like her doctor said to do, then thought again of her conversation with the dean of the UNC journalism school.

"Are you sure, Mary, that you won't reconsider taking the job?" he asked. "You're the most qualified applicant we have, and we'd love to have you join our staff."

Mary had told him her decision was firm, that she had decided to concentrate her career in another direction. She hadn't mentioned she was pregnant.

Mary was turning to drop the glass into the wastebasket when she heard the distant growl of Woodrow's hunting horn. She was startled, the slick glass slipped from her fingers and fell to the floor. The glass bounced once, skittered on the rim, then shattered.

"Damn, damn, damn!" Mary cried, stamping her foot. The shards of glass split the lamplight into colors. She put her hands to her face, hearing the baying of the hounds begin as they answered Woodrow. Another blast of the horn. Mary felt rage swell the blood vessels in her temples.

My God! I thought that fuss ended last month. I can't stand to listen to it tonight. Not tonight. I wish Jeffery were here.

Mary stared at the shattered glass. For a moment, she had an insane impulse to swallow the fragments. She covered her mouth with her hand to stifle an urge to retch. The day before while paring potatoes, she'd had an impulse to thrust the small blade into her abdomen.

Now calm down, she told herself. Take another breath. Dr. Spock says all pregnant women have such thoughts occasionally. She patted her belly. Oh, I do want you, baby. I want to hold you and hug you, give you baths and watch you grow big as Daddy. Things are just mixed up right now. Please forgive Mommy for being so silly.

Mary stared again at the shards of glass on the floor. She wished they would disappear, sink into the floor, melt—anything that would not force her to get out the vacuum cleaner and broom. Even small tasks were becoming insurmountable.

Again Mary heard the long notes of Woodrow's horn. She felt tears sting her eyes, but shook her head to stop them. No, you are a grown woman. You're not going to cry again. You're being silly. Most women would be happy to be pregnant with all we have to share.

Mary crossed the kitchen to the utility closet. With her hand on the doorknob, she listened to the hounds bay in unison. Their song told of wildness—a mile traveled, but many more to gain. She swung open the door, the hinges protesting with a long squeal.

The squeal was the exact pitch of the infant on the hillside in Iowa. The cry was pitiful but demanding. In the darkness of the closet, Mary saw the image of the washerwoman in her wrinkled dress, her hair limp with perspiration. She smiled at Mary, tiredly but sincerely, lifting her hand to show a photo of a schoolgirl, her young eyes bright and clear, her chin thrust defiantly forward. Their resemblance had not totally faded.

"Welcome, sister," the woman whispered. "You have lost only what we all lose in time. But you have gained membership in the great sisterhood."

A shiver started at the base of Mary's spine, sweeping up her back and across her shoulders. She closed her eyes and hugged her arms to her bosom, stepped back from the vision.

"No. I am not like you," Mary shouted. "I will never be like you!"

A shard of glass cut deeply into Mary's heel. She gasped and jerked up her foot, the chunk falling from her flesh and tinkling on the floor. She felt no pain, only looked dumbly as blood splattered against the tiles.

Mary waited on the front porch for Jeffery, felt a throbbing begin in her heel and swim over her ankle. The blood stopped flowing and congealed in a dark puddle around her foot. Against the dark horizon she stared at the curve of the palm tree. Several times, cars passed slowly, radios blaring. In the dim light from the streetlight, the dead grass on the lawn was visible. When finally Jeffery's car lights appeared in the drive, Mary hobbled down the steps to meet him.

"Hello, baby," he said, locking the car door. "Sorry I'm late, but the—"

Mary hushed him by putting her fingers against his lips. "Jeffery," she began in a monotone. "Jeffery, if you love me . . . if you truly love me . . ."

Ellis doodled with a pencil on a sheet of paper. He drew spirals, a stick dog, a crude naked woman, finally erasing the woman's figure. Mississippi wasn't the high country of the Rockies, and the more he thought about it, the less he liked getting linked to another piece of land.

"Just think about it, Ellis," Nadean said. "I think he would move down there if you went. You know how he feels about you."

"They really have alligators down there?" he asked, still not looking up.

"Benson said so and he was there. Big ones he said."

Ellis sketched an alligator. He drew the animal with a wide gaping mouth.

"Benson said it warm down there, too," Nadean continued. "Said you can go 'round in short sleeves all the time."

Ellis drew a round bullet hole in the alligator's head. He stared at the drawing. "I wouldn't mind shooting me an alligator," he said.

Nadean crossed the room and stood over Ellis. He covered his drawings with his hands. "Ellis, I know you got the itch to wander, and I can't blame you. Crazy as this place is getting, I'm a mind to go, too. But baby, you got to have something you can carry with you that's home. Something strong that can bring you back if you get in trouble." She reached and lifted his chin with one hand. "Ellis, I don't know if this is home 'round here no more. I'm mixed up. But I do know that we family. Me and you and Woodrow, we family. Maybe if we went south and started over, it would be better. Then you could wander the ends of the earth and every night I'd put a candle in the window that you could look for and see. It would be the brightest star in the sky."

"I'd like to make me a belt from an alligator," Ellis said, refusing to look up. "There ain't much in the world that can whip an alligator."

Nadean stitched a hole in Woodrow's overalls with loop after loop until the patch was thick like a callus. One moment she thought the idea of moving south was a good one, but then her mind would change and she'd fear leaving would just be one more time in her life that she had run away.

The hounds could be heard as a low murmur from the ridge. Run on dogs, she thought. Run clear 'round the world if you need to, till you find me a place where a palm tree be welcome in the middle of oaks.

"It's deep, but clean," said Gail Chandler, a doctor who lived in the subdivision. "You don't need any stitches, but it's sure going to be sore for a few days." She smiled at Mary, who reclined on the sofa. Jeffery stood behind the doctor. Gail wrapped the wound carefully.

"I want you to get in bed and rest," Gail ordered. "I've given you a very mild sedative that will help you sleep. I'll stop by again tomorrow afternoon and check for any signs of infection." She closed her bag, then patted Mary's knee. Jeffery walked her to the door.

"I really appreciate you coming out this late," Jeffery said.

"Don't mention it. We're friends." Gail lowered her voice. "Jeffery, I'm really concerned about Mary's blood pressure. It's too high."

Jeffery blew out a long breath. "She's been so upset lately about this problem with Bunce. She can't sleep. Cries a lot. I don't know what to do."

"Well, she's got to settle down. Stress and babies aren't good together. I'd hate to see her miscarry."

Jeffery's eyes widened as if he had been slapped. Gail said goodnight and left.

Jeffery lifted Mary and carried her to their bed. He fluffed her pillow and covered her, then kissed her nose. "I want you to sleep now."

"Jeffery, this craziness around here has got to stop. I can't keep—"

Jeffery put his finger to her lips. "Shhhh. I said go to sleep. Things are going to be straightened out. I promise you." He turned out the light and closed the door.

Jeffery sat at the kitchen table for several minutes, sipping a gin and thinking. When a person has a cancer, doctors cut it out before it has time to spread. If it is allowed to spread too much, it will kill you. That palm tree is a cancer in our community and it's spreading. It has to be cut out, and it has to be done now. If it is cut out, life will become normal again.

Jeffery waited a few minutes longer until he knew Mary was sleeping. Then he dialed Dack's number. They talked for a couple of minutes. Then Jeffery called Derrick, and next, Tom.

Upon the ridge, the hounds ran aimlessly, in search of a fresh scent. In years past, the trails left by wild animals were so plentiful it was all Woodrow could do to call the hounds in when it came time to return home. Tonight, the dogs bayed loud their frustration, circling Woodrow as he walked the crest, occasionally picking up an old scent to find it peter out. Woodrow urged them with his horn in vain. Three times he stumbled over new survey paths.

Suddenly, one of the young dogs caught a fresh scent, threw back his head, and bayed the deep voice of pursuit. The other hounds fell in, Woodrow lifted his horn and rent the air with one short, powerful blast.

Woodrow had run only a hundred yards when he sensed that something was different. The cry of the hounds did not follow the usual zigzag path that a rabbit or raccoon would use in flight. The hunt did not wind through the bramble and briers on the south side of the ridge, nor did it turn toward the river. The prey seemed to run a straight path toward town, as if the animal were following one of the surveyor trails. Woodrow stopped and listened, then seconds later heard the hounds bay long and deep—they must have treed—then snarls and the high-pitched pained cry of an animal. Down the slope he raced toward the snarls, until his lantern shone on his hounds standing noses together over a still form.

Woodrow jerked the dogs back, then shone his beam on the mangled body of a tabby cat. The cat wore a flea collar. The hounds whimpered, blood and fur stuck to their snouts, stupefied over their first kill.

Woodrow stared at the body for several moments. The wildness is gone from here. He recalled Benson saying, "Our hills are dead, little brother."

Woodrow raised his horn and blew the long blast that turned the hounds toward town. In his mind, he pictured a small farm in delta country, unsettled land far from the nearest home.

Nadean was sitting in a rocking chair, humming softly while mending another hole in a pair of Woodrow's overalls, when she was startled by a sharp rap on the front door. She glanced at the clock and saw that it read ten till ten. Who the world that be this time'a night? Nadean stuck the needle through the cuff of the overalls and laid them on the arm of the chair. She was straining

to stand when she saw Ellis come from his bedroom and head for
the door.

"If it Benson, tell him Woodrow still out hunting," Nadean
called. She heard the creak of the door, then a curious silence that
lasted several seconds. "What ya'll want?" finally Nadean heard
Ellis say in a tight voice. She heaved to her feet and walked until
she could see.

Jeffery Stewert stood with several men from the subdivision.
Nadean felt her heart squeeze. Ellis's back partly shielded Jeffery,
but from the way one of his shoulders stopped, she knew he held
something heavy. Nadean hurried over. When she peered around
Ellis's shoulder, the men shuffled their feet and coughed. Nadean
saw that Jeffery held a small chain saw in his hand. She stared into
his eyes; he held her gaze. In the silence, Nadean realized she no
longer heard Woodrow's hounds baying from the ridge.

"I asked what ya'll want here this late at night," Ellis demanded. "What the hell you doing with that piss-ant chain saw,
too?"

Jeffery ignored Ellis. "Nadean," he began, "the time has come
to cure what's happening to this community. That palm tree is a
cancer. It's destroying the peace and happiness we have here, and
it has to go. It has to go now."

"The law gonna tell us if it has to go," Nadean said. "Woodrow appealed, and what the judge says next month, we'll do."

Jeffery shook his head. "The law was already passed, Nadean.
Property's being damaged. Mary's so upset, she may miscarry.
The palm has to come down tonight."

Nadean looked from face to face, each man holding her gaze—
the same people she had talked with over good wine and coffee,
discussed harmony while ending hunger and the problems of the
world. She closed her eyes and pictured the rich delta soil Benson
had described earlier that night. It sounded good—land far from
tar roads and other houses, fields where a body could shout and no

one would know it from the wind.

"You assholes wouldn't be here if Woodrow was home," Ellis said. "Bunch of cowards gang up when you think no one can stop you." Ellis curled one fist.

Nadean put her hand on his shoulder. She shook him. "Stay quiet, Ellis. This mess always been my doing. You stay quiet and out of the way."

Jeffery touched the saw with his free hand. "I hate this, Nadean, but it's got to be done. A month from now, this will be forgotten and everyone can be friends again. But it's got to be done." He turned and looked at the palm. "If you or the boy wants to cut it, fine. Otherwise, I'll do it."

"You see a boy, you kiss his ass," Ellis said, his face in a sneer.

"I said stay out of this, Ellis," Nadean shouted. She pushed him backwards. "Go study for them exams and keep your mouth shut."

Nadean turned back to Jeffery. "You do what you feel you gotta do, mister. Me and Woodrow and Ellis, we be leaving here soon." She touched her breast. "It's all right here what I need. I know that now. I can carry that with me anywhere."

Jeffery nodded. He turned with the other men.

"And Jeffery," Nadean called. He turned back.

"Damn you and Mary and the eagles and those fancy dinner parties. I was always thinking that, anyway."

Ellis watched the men stomp down the stairs. He watched Nadean walk out onto the porch, then, step by step, follow until she stood several yards onto the lawn. He wished Woodrow kept a gun. He walked from the house onto the porch, his quick breath white in the cold air.

Dogs. He heard dogs barking from afar—not the sound of hunt, but yelps, like Woodrow's hounds sounded when he was herding them home. The sounds were low, the dogs still on the ridge, but second by second, he knew Woodrow was coming. Ellis saw Nadean turn her face toward the ridge; she also knew

Woodrow had abandoned the hunt.

Oh, shit, Ellis thought. Excitement and dread filled his gut.

Nadean turned and spied Ellis on the porch. She cocked her head again at the sound of the approaching dogs. "Ellis," she shouted. "Woodrow's coming early. Go call Benson. Tell him he better get over here."

Ellis dialed the number, then waited while it rang six times. Margo answered, and he asked for Benson, heard a sleepy voice come on at the other end.

"Benson, this is Ellis," he shouted into the mouthpiece. "You better get over here. Some men from the subdivision are trying to cut down the palm tree and Woodrow's coming down the ridge. There's gonna be—"

Ellis heard a click as Benson slammed the receiver down.

Ellis hurried back to the yard where he stood beside Nadean. He saw that her cheeks were wet, and for a moment thought of charging the men. As if sensing that, Nadean grasped his arm.

"This better, Ellis. Let them cut it. We ain't, and won't. Now we'll go from here. Make a new home."

Ellis wanted to laugh at Jeffery's attempts to start the brand-new chain saw. He jerked at the starter cord, but the handle pulled through his fingers. He jerked it harder, this time nearly dropping the saw. He pumped the throttle, then jerked again, the engine turned but didn't catch.

"Choke it," Derrick said. Jeffery pushed in the choke knob. He jerked the cord again and the engine fired and sputtered, then died.

The hounds drew closer. Ellis peered toward the ridge. He saw that Nadean also searched the darkness. "Please, God, don't let him get here," Ellis heard her mumble.

Jeffery adjusted the choke and jerked the cord. The engine fired, caught this time, and a cloud of oily, blue smoke surrounded the men. The others stood back while Jeffery revved the engine, his face tight as if he feared the whirling chain. He took a stance at one side of the palm, feet set wide in the sand, revved the engine again, squinted his eyes, and whacked the trunk of the palm.

If Jeffery hadn't held such a death grip on the saw, he might have cut off his own head, for the chain saw kicked back from the wood and only chewed a shallow wound. Jeffery glanced at his friends, set his feet again, then swung the saw against the tree the way one might an ax. Again, the the saw kicked backwards. Jeffery stared at the saw, then at the slight damage he had done to the tree. He released the throttle and let the engine idle.

"Do it easy," Ellis heard Dack shout. "Put the chain against the trunk, then give it gas."

The dogs were loud. Ellis heard a blast from Woodrow's horn, commanding them to stay in pack. He figured they were less than a quarter mile from home. The men looked anxiously toward the ridge, sensing now that trouble was coming. Jeffery inserted the saw bar into the shallow cut and slowly pressed the throttle. The chain teeth binded and the engine stalled.

"Let me do it," Derrick demanded. Jeffery stared at the saw, then handed it to him.

"No. There ain't nobody going to do it," a loud voice called from the shadows at the side of the house. Everyone turned and looked toward where the voice had come. "Best thing you can do is throw that chain saw in the pool and go the hell on home," the voice called again.

"Who says?" Derrick called out.

"I do."

Ellis watched as a form stepped out of the darkness of the side yard into the light that spilled from the front porch. At first, Ellis had trouble even making out the shape of a man, so well did he blend into the shadows and dark contours of night, but as the shape drew closer, he recognized Mack Lupo.

"Lord Jesus," Nadean gasped, her mouth open as if she stared at a ghost.

Everyone stared, the men around the base of the palm, Ellis, Nadean, several subdivision residents and townspeople who had gathered at the edge of the yard, curious over what was happening.

Mack was dressed in the jungle khaki he'd brought home from the war, his face and hands darkened with grease and soot. His mouth was slightly open, and Ellis noticed that even his teeth had been darkened. Except for the sound of the hounds, all was silent for several seconds.

"Just who do you think you are?" Derrick finally asked.

"Somebody that's lived here his whole life. Somebody that ain't going to stand around and see his home taken away." Mack took several more steps toward the men. "Somebody that ain't going to let you cut down that tree."

Derrick looked at Jeffery, then at Tom. He licked his lips. "Well, Mr. Rambo, I don't know what your game is, but I don't think you can stop us."

Mack looked at Nadean. "Nadean, these men are trespassing. By law you can order them off your land. If you ask and they don't leave, we can use force."

"Mack, please just let them go ahead." Nadean sobbed now, tears dripping from where they converged on her chin. "I don't care no more. I just want to see this mess ended."

The hounds were close. Above the yelp and cry of the dogs, Ellis heard what sounded like a siren approaching. He wished Benson would hurry.

Jeffery studied Mack's clothes. "Look at that red paint on your trousers. You're the one who's been causing all the trouble, aren't you?" His voice went shrill. "You're the one that's made my wife so upset."

"If anyone's to blame for trouble around here, it's you people," Mack answered.

"My wife . . ." Jeffery shouted. "God damn you." He grabbed the saw from Derrick and pulled repeatedly at the cord. "My wife—she—you can't stop me." He swore when the saw wouldn't start.

A dog bayed, the old bitch entered the circle of light, her tail wagged at the sight of people. "Oh, God," Nadean moaned. The siren was close. A car squealed to a stop and Benson jumped out. "Thank God," cried Nadean.

Woodrow came on long strides up the hill, his face a mask of wonder and confusion. Jeffery pulled at the saw, pulled again, it caught, was revved, he bent toward the tree—BAM!

Mack held aloft a .45, smoke curling from the end of the barrel. "You ain't cutting that tree," he screamed.

"What's wrong?" Woodrow shouted as he crested the hill, turned in a circle, wide eyes noting the gash in the palm, Nadean crying, his brother running toward him, a man in war paint holding aloft a smoking gun.

The scene was like going back in time, Ellis would always remember, like returning many years to the day when he saw Woodrow hugging the chinaberry tree. As the big man turned in a circle, his eyes went shiny like mirrors, his mouth opened and saliva glinted on his lip. He stopped and stared at Mack.

"We got to stop them, Woodrow," Mack said. "You and me can stop them."

Ellis stepped closer to Woodrow. Jeffery jerked at the cord, the saw sputtered again and died. BAM! Mack shot into the air. "You ain't cutting that God damn tree." He stared at Woodrow. "Tell them, Woodrow. Order them off your land."

Ellis watched Woodrow squint his eyes. "No!" Woodrow shouted. "Nooooo!" He opened his eyes and stared at Mack, then at the tree, at Nadean who sobbed, at Benson. He stepped backwards. Ellis saw another place reflected in Woodrow's eyes. "I can't do it, Lieutenant," Woodrow shouted. "I can't do it."

Jeffery pulled at the cord again, and the engine roared to life. Mack leveled his heavy pistol with two hands and squeezed off a round. The bullet kicked up a plume of sand only a few feet from

Jeffery. Jeffery leaped backwards and dropped the saw. He stared incredulously at Mack, the amazement in his eyes changing to fear.

The saw vibrated upon the sand. Mack sighted again. The next bullet knocked the saw to the edge of the beach and silenced the engine. Another shot kicked it several yards onto the grass. Ellis watched fire leap a foot from the barrel, the sound slapped against his ears.

Woodrow squinted his eyes again, put his hands over his ears. "I can't do it, Lieutenant. I just can't." An animal cry came from his lips. Ellis stared. Mack kept his aim on the saw, but turned his head to stare. The men gathered at the palm stared. Woodrow whimpered, covered his face with his hands.

Nadean locked eyes with Ellis, and held the gaze for a moment. She leaped and grabbed the hot barrel of the big pistol and pulled it down to stop Mack from shooting again, twisted the gun in an attempt to pull it from his hands. His finger still lay against the trigger, and when Nadean snatched, the gun discharged. The slug passed through her belly, shattered her lower spine, then exited in a spray of bone fragments and blood. Her mouth opened but no words came, she let go of the pistol and sank to the ground.

Everyone froze for a moment. Wherever Woodrow's memory had taken him, he snapped to and returned to aid Nadean. He knelt over her and cradled her head in the crook of his arm. He pushed a sprig of hair from her face. She tried to speak again, but only a pink bubble came up. She smiled sadly.

"I didn't mean to—oh, God!" Mack stammered for words. "She grabbed the barrel—I never thought—"

Jeffery and Tom rushed over; Dack raced to call an ambulance. The siren was loud, brakes squealed. People shouted and pointed. The blue light flashed upon the beach, the radio crackled as the patrolman called for backup. The wail of another distant siren began.

"Oh God, oh God," Jeffery shouted over and over. He squeezed in beside Mack; the two men's eyes caught and hung. Woodrow looked up, his eyes suddenly very clear and intent, and with one fluid motion he rose, stepped across Nadean, and caught both men by their throats. He grunted once as he lifted until both hung from arm's length. The two flailed and kicked, faces turning purple. Benson pushed through the crowd, shouted and jerked at his brother's arms, but Woodrow didn't see him, saw only those struggling in his hands.

"Woodrow," Ellis screamed. "Let them go, Woodrow. Let them down."

Woodrow stood erect, arms locked, his eyes on the men. He seemed to hear and feel nothing. Mack and Jeffery struggled less. From the corner of his eye, Ellis saw Derrick pick up a rock from the beach, raise it, and start for Woodrow. Ellis crouched, then met him and buried his fist in the man's gut, heard him gasp, then bend double.

The state patrolman passed Ellis running. His nightstick was out, and with one well-placed lick, he buckled Woodrow's knees. The second blow to his knees brought the big man down.

Nadean died in the ambulance on the way to Memorial Hospital. Three days later, a tree pruning company removed the palm under orders from the county.

Two months later, when Ellis could bring himself to call from a pay phone in Phoenix, he learned that Woodrow had died in his sleep soon after his admittance to Dorothea Dix Hospital. He was buried in the family plot beside his mother and father.

llis turned away from the chiseled entrance sign to the subdivision and walked the short distance to Woodrow's old house. He had expected change, but was still shocked to find the watermelon field sliced into lots with three new houses already completed.

Woodrow's house had been renovated, the white boards covered with cedar paneling that allowed it to blend in nicely with the newer homes. The front porch had been enclosed to make a room. Ellis slowly climbed the hill toward a high redwood fence.

The house was dark, shades drawn, so Ellis swung open the heavy gate. No beach—the sand and shells covered with a smooth pad of concrete, a diving board mounted at the end of the pool where the palm had grown. The pink flamingos had been replaced with an inflated plastic swan lying on its side in the water; an empty wine bottle sat in the middle of a wrought-iron patio table. Ellis closed the gate, returning the family their privacy.

Ellis walked the road that wound through the subdivision. He paused in front of the Stewerts' house.

Still here, he thought. They bought a new mailbox that looks like their house. A new Volvo wagon sat beside the older Volvo sedan. Another room had been added. A plastic Big Wheels tricycle was parked on the clipped lawn.

Ellis caught the odor of coffee. Oak Hills was waking up. Traffic would begin soon. He walked from the subdivision and headed out of town to where the black community had stood. Many of the old tenant houses had been torn down, but the church still stood, the cemetery now badly grown over with weeds. The billboard out front contained the name of a pastor that Ellis didn't know.

Ellis found Nadean's headstone under a latticework of ivy vines. He sat down on the cool ground, took out his pocketknife, and began stripping away the vines. He wiped off the dirt that had collected in the engraved letters spelling her name. Ellis enjoyed the quiet of the graveyard. He heard only a woodpecker hammering a dead limb.

A car drove past, disturbing the woodpecker, who flew into deeper woods. In the rear window of the car, Ellis saw the face of a child. The boy waved to him. Nearby, chiseled in the bark of a sycamore tree, were the initials of two children. A new generation had begun to explore Oak Hills, would wade her creeks, climb the ridge to admire the view, and search what was left of the forest. Few would know, or care, that the number of frogs had diminished, the deer fled, the tobacco fields long fallow.

Ellis untied the laces on his sneakers, shook out the few pebbles, worked his toes against the cool grass. Once he had paused to
rest his feet underneath a red cliff in Utah where the remains of an
ancient Indian village stood—the squat clay hovels now home to
lizards and scorpions. At a marker commemorating the Oregon
Trail, he had stopped only briefly to scan the tale of the thousands
of people who had walked that dry path in search of home. He
had rested his feet for a month once in the mobile home of a
young woman in Pueblo, listening each night with growing
boredom to her tales of the damp, green childhood she remembered from Vermont. Ellis rubbed the tendons in his feet and
smiled. A good pair of restless feet could keep a man alive forever.

Ellis removed the plastic sack from his shirt pocket. He
pinched off one corner, then slowly shook a handful of powdery
dirt onto Nadean's grave. Off a rural roadside in lower Mississippi he had dug beneath the grass to collect rich, unturned soil
that lay out of sight of the nearest house.

Ellis felt his stomach rumble. So, what now, he wondered?
Maybe I'll head over and see if Miss Penny still makes ham
bisquits. Might even stop for a moment and see Enzor—the old
shit. Then? I don't know. I heard that in Maine they hire people
to work summers in the fishing industry.

Ellis opened the catch to his rucksack. He removed a bundle of
old rags and carefully unwrapped the edges. He held aloft Woodrow's hunting horn. The lip of the horn was chipped, the brass
mouthpiece tarnished, but it otherwise looked the same. Ellis
nestled the horn in the fescue grass covering Nadean's grave. It
looked natural there, like dead wood fallen from a tree. On
impulse, Ellis lifted the horn once more. He put the mouthpiece
to his lips and blew.

The unused horn only rattled. Ellis sucked down air, puckered
his lips again, and blew hard. His wind swelled in the mouth of
the horn, a low blast spilled out and grew slowly till it blocked

out the drone of cars, the songs of mourning doves. His salute lifted above the treetops, rolled up the denuded ridge, echoed off the walls of a house, and reverberated with volume across the heartland.